ISLOM KARIMOV

UZBEKISTAN ALONG THE ROAD OF DEEPENING ECONOMIC REFORM

Tashkent - "UZBEKISTON" - 1995

65.9(5У)
К 25

ISBN 5-640-01909-3

К $\frac{0605010404-80}{М\,351\,(04)\,95}$ 95

© Издательство "ЎЗБЕКИСТОН", 1995

FOREWORD

Independent Uzbekistan is travelling along the road chosen by the nation, along the road of open and free market relations, and along the road of building a just society and a strong law-governed democratic state. The state we are building belongs to the world civilization and is based on the experiences of other advanced nations in building their statehood and on common social values.

There are deep economic and socio-political transformations currently taking place in Uzbekistan; their theoretical and practical programmes have been thoroughly described in their author's well-known works "Uzbekistan: the Road of Independence and Progress", "Uzbekistan: its Own Model of Transition to a Market Economy", "Our Objective is a Free and Prospering Fatherland", "Honesty and Selflessness and Basic Criteria of Our Activity" and "Basic Principles of Social, Political and Economic Development of Uzbekistan".

These works examine major tasks facing a newly independent state, among them the reform of the country's economic and social life, democratization of economic relations and high spirituality. These are called upon to lay a foundation of prosperity for our state.

This manual calls readers' attention to some of the conclusions drawn from experience gained after proclamations of our country's independence, tells about socio-economic changes in the life of the nation, and provides deep analysis of transformations in the mentality of the people.

A completely new theory and practical moves in state structuring and building-up of the economy advanced by the Republic of Uzbekistan attract the attention of leading world economists and politologists, and they are given broader coverage in the manual. On the basis of analysis of the results of the first stage of economic reform — the stage of introduction of different forms of ownership — and the analysis of achievements in this field; the manual examines the tasks facing a newly independent Republic at the second stage of reform, outlines new priorities, and proposes ways for the solution of these still more complicated tasks.

The manual consists of two parts. The first part, called "Results and Lessons of the First Stage of Economic Reform", deals with problems of shaping strategy, ways of implementation of economic reform and establishment of legal foundation of market relations. It also tells about privatization of state property, formation of a multi-structural economy, about the course of reform in agriculture, and the establishment of agrarian relations of a new type. These are the questions widely discussed in the manual along with particular stress on institutional transformations, i.e. setting up new organizations and establishments corresponding to market relations and liquidation of the administrative-command system of management.

The central issue of analysis in this part of the manual is the process of price liberalization, establishment of a market infrastructure, problems of liberalization of external economic activity, and joining the world economic community.

The tasks and objectives facing economic reform, creation of decent living and working conditions for the population of the country, rehabilitation of the nation's moral and ethic values, and problems of securing economic and socio-political stability in the country are given deep and thorough consideration.

The second part of the manual is entitled "Tasks and Priorities of the Second Stage of Economic Reform" and deals with basic tasks in the sphere of economic advancement of our country. These include deepening of privatization process and introduction of a competitive environment ensuring macro-economic stability, consolidation of national currency, carrying out deep structural transformations, and shaping a democratic state with strong social guarantees. The solution of these tasks requires the elaboration of fundamental theoretical and practical basis. The principal objective of the second part is to identify directions of activities of prior significance in this sphere.

This manual is an important aid for students of higher and special secondary educational institutions and will prove helpful for researchers, economists, executive officers, production managers, and entrepreneurs studying closely new trends of developments and the laws of market economy.

INTRODUCTION

The newly independent state of Uzbekistan situated in the heart of Asian continent has been establishing itself on the political map of the world. Progressive changes taking place in Uzbekistan, its tremendous natural resources, production, scientific, technical and intellectual potential and a unique national and cultural heritage turn this country into an attractive site for foreign politicians, businessmen and common people interested in the history and present-day life of our people.

Uzbekistan plays an ever-growing role in the changing geopolitical structure. Both its CIS partners and prestigious international organizations, of which we are full-fledged members, are compelled to take into account Uzbekistan's opinion and its stance. As a result of the consistent peace-loving policy conducted by Uzbekistan, its role of a guarantor of peace and stability in the Central Asian region has been considerably consolidated.

Millions of people of different ethnic groups and religious belief living in peace and accord in this ancient land of plenty feel their destiny and future to be closely connected with Uzbekistan. Having achieved their independence and throwing off the yoke of totalitarian regime, the people of Uzbekistan inscribe a new page in their centuries-old history through their selfless labour.

The years of independence have been a time of objective cognition of the past and culture for the people of Uzbekistan. It has been a time of comprehension of the role assigned us in the world community and history. Free from ideological indoctrination these have been the years of sober analysis of reasons, which threw a potentially rich Republic down to the abyss of crisis, the years of searching for the means for its soonest elimination.

The years of independence have been a time of active state and political structuring of a newly democratic state. This is a time of spiritual revival and growing feeling of self-identity. This is a time filled with the spirit of freedom and confidence in one's own potentials and bright future of the country and its people.

Most importantly, the first years of independence are a period of active search for the road of the Republic's own development and aspiration to turn our Motherland into a free, strong and prospering country.

State independence opened up broad opportunities for economic and social progress, for its cultural and spiritual renovation.

Circumstances had it that from the very outset Uzbekistan had to independently solve the most acute problems inherited by a hypertrophied and one-sided economy with deformities in the utilization of natural and mineral resources, in the development and distribution of productive forces, price-formation and the population consumption structure; to independently identify mechanisms and forms of transforming administrative-planning relations into market economic relations; look for optimal ways for integrating with the system of world economic ties and establishing inter-state economic relations.

All of this required the search for our own road of renovation of society and socio-economic progress. The road we have selected is aimed at shaping a socially-oriented market economy based on all-round consideration of world experience, as well as living conditions, traditions, customs and our people's way of life.

The road we have chosen is based on a constitutional foundation and to the greatest extent possible meets the interests of Uzbekistan's entire population.

Namely such a road serves as a guarantee for securing decent life for the people of Uzbekistan, ensures the development of national traditions and culture and revival of spiritual and moral values.

The final objective is the construction of a strong democratic law-governed state and secular society with a stable socially-oriented market economy and open foreign policy.

A pivotal line of state structuring in the Republic of Uzbekistan is a consistent and purposeful proceeding along its own road with due consideration of both the experiences of other countries, which have lived through hardships of self-establishment, and the specific peculiarities of the Republic and mentality of the people.

These provisions of principle, organically merging together like two brooks into a powerful stream which gradually, day by day, gains strength and experience, will have to be channelled into renovation and progress of our society and the State.

The five well-known key principles form the basis for the realization of this policy of radical economic reform during the transition period.

These principles have passed the test of time and their efficiency has been confirmed in practice. They have been approved by the world public and, more importantly, have been accepted and approved by the nation. Currently the realization of these principles secures socio-political stability and persistent advancement towards the implementation of market relations in the Republic. Hence, we are committed to be further guided by these principles.

We have sufficiently revealed the full essence of these principles, which in brief are as follows:

First, complete deideologization of economy. Economy should prevail over politics and constitute its inner content, to be more precise, the economy and problems of its further development form the core of our current policy.

Second, the state should play the role of a chief reformer during the complicated transition period. It should initiate the process of reform in the interests of the nation, identify priorities of economic progress and elaborate and consistently implement a policy of radical transformations in economy, social sphere, and public and political life of our sovereign state.

Third, the entire process of renovation and progress should be based on a legal foundation. Only then tangible results of economic transformations may be expected and made irreversible when they are founded on adjusted and practically applicable laws.

Fourth, consideration of the real demographic situation and the existing living standard of the population transition to market relations should be associated with the implementation of preventive moves for the social protection of people. Only a strong and efficient mechanism of social protection and guarantees may secure dynamic advancement towards market economy with simultaneous maintenance of socio-political stability.

And, **fifth**, the establishment of new economic market relations should be introduced with careful consideration and stage by stage.

All these principles are equally vital for the implementation of successful democratic and economic reforms. Nevertheless, the principle of gradual, stage by stage transition to market economy deserves particular significance. This is one of the leading principles. It determines the entire inner logic, dynamism and the nature of economic reform.

More than once, we underlined that it was vital to advance step by step towards the final objective. The establishment of a corresponding legal foundation, market infrastructure, training of personnel capable to work under new conditions is a time-consuming process.

It is extremely vital to change the mentality of the people and break dominating stereotypes. Failure to convince people of the need for renovation and transformation of society, failure to change driving forces and human values, motivation of labour and behaviour mean to doom reform to failure and there can be no talk about creating a new society and establishing principally new relations.

We have made a simple choice — to consistently advance towards market economy stage by stage, i.e. evolutionary not by great leaps or revolutionary destruction. Each stage constitutes a link in the implementation of a strategy of reform in progress. It has to be constantly compared with strategic priorities, reflect the gradual nature of their implementation and serve as a barometer, determining the correctness of the chosen course and, as needed introduce necessary corrections. The strategic line is the principal guiding line for identifying stages and determining their objectives, tasks and priorities.

Any forced advancement towards market without corresponding preparation results in a failure, in critical deterioration of events, in the break-up of existing structures and economic links and, as a consequence, in the collapse of economy, social sphere and discreditation of the very idea of market relations. In other words, it is the road that leads a country, which had chosen it, to complete destruction, to the brink of precipice and to social violence.

The implementation of the principle of gradual transition to market relations presupposes careful consideration of all inherited progressive tendencies, on the one hand, and clear identification of major stages of reform, determining concrete objectives and mechanisms for their achievement, on the other.

Popular saying has it: never destroy the old house before you build a new one. It is unforgivable to neglect what could be used in the interests of economic reform during transition to market relations and make this process more efficient and less painful.

In the first place this is related to determining the place and role of the state within the system of economic relations. Denial of state regulation of economy in yet volatile conditions of self-regulation under strong impact of demand and offer with no visible signs of free competition and limited range of external links provokes deepening of crisis, price rise and higher inflation rate.

The guarantee of success is a continuity of stages in the implementation of reform. **The final objective — shaping of a democratic society with free market economy — should be embodied in each stage of advancement towards it.** Formation of each stage must entail the sequence of objectives and their subsequent achievement. Only realistically outlined tasks for each stage, a clearly elaborated mechanism of their solution secure forward movement towards the chosen goal. This provides an opportunity to concentrate efforts and resources on meeting the tasks and identifying the most significant priorities and subdue their achievement to the global process of economic reform.

Every next stage starts after completion of the previous stage and creation of necessary prerequisites for the subsequent one. Economic reform will have to gradually, step by step form genuine market relation mechanisms which are not switched on all at once, but adjusted gradually to make them operational.

By mentally preparing people at each stage and convincing them of the advantages of the new system through practical results, we may succeed in the implementation of reform to the end and build a society with advanced economic structure and efficient social relations.

Today we have found corresponding approaches, dynamic rhythm of work and gained certain helpful experience. Time has come to sum up the first results and identify tasks and priorities for the next stage.

Actually, we have completed a titanic comprehensive preparatory work of adapting national economy and psychology of the people to new conditions and realities.

The primary achievement of our policy is the broad support of reform by all residents of the Republic. This instills confidence in the success of reform.

However, without revealing the causes keeping back the advancement of reform and without eliminating barriers on its way we may fall into a prolonged lingering process of reformation, which case is fraud with devaluation of the essence of reform. It may loose its major advantage — igniting new impulses, stimuli and strong motivation for changes. This is something which cannot be permitted.

Through analysing what has already been accomplished, we consider the adoption of a new strategy for deepening economic reform on a qualitatively new stage and identify its major tasks and objectives to be our current task of primary importance.

Part 1

RESULTS AND LESSONS OF THE FIRST STAGE OF ECONOMIC REFORM

A qualitatively new stage in the implementation of economic reform started with the introduction of national currency into circulation in Uzbekistan. Today we can confidently declare that we have gone through the initial, the most difficult, stage. It was the stage which laid the foundation of the entire process of economic reform. It has passed the test of time and there is every ground to state that it fulfilled successfully its function.

The first stage of the transition period indicated the difficulties of the reform process and at the same time identified unstandard and inordinary approaches to the revival of natural economic relations.

The first stage was generally directed towards the establishment of a legal foundation for a new economic system, formation and consolidation of statehood and elimination of old stereotypes of thinking. This stage had to solve and solved the task of creating a reliable foundation for a new system.

What are the main results of the first stage, what has been accomplished from what was planned and what are the conclusion to be drawn from the analysis of the past experience? A complete and objective answer to this question will provide an opportunity to better understand the historical significance of accomplishments and fairly evaluate the progress we have made along the road of formation of market relations. This will also provide an opportunity to derive proper lessons from the past to avoid deviations from the chosen course at subsequent steps and stages of reform and renovation of our society.

1.1. MECHANISM OF FORMATION OF ECONOMIC REFORM'S STRATEGY AND COURSE

The principal result of the initial stage of radical transformations is that we have managed to elaborate and practically implement our own model of formation of reform's strategy and course.

The choice of strategy — an exceptionally responsible and delicate matter — is of crucial importance for the entire process of reform. Efficient moves in the field of economic reform may hardly be undertaken without general strategy and without visualizing the final objective.

Determination of the final objective of socio-economic transformations serves as the starting point for the modern strategy of form. We have underlined more than once that transition from centralized administrative-command to market system does not presuppose the modernization or improvement of the old economic mechanism but transition from one qualitative condition into another. This means replacement of certain economic relations and organizational-administrative structures by different ones.

The strategic objectives in the field of economic reform outlined on the basis of Uzbekistan's interests in achieving political and economic independence, building up its national statehood and establishment of a solid material foundation are as follows:

1. Stage-by-stage shaping of socially-oriented market economy, establishment of a powerful and dynamically developing economic system ensuring further growth of national wealth and creating decent living and working conditions for the people.

2. Creation of a multi-structural economy, elimination of alienation of man from property, ensuring state protection of private ownership as the basis for all-round development of initiative and entrepreneurship.

3. Provision of broad economic liberties to enterprises and citizens, denial of state's direct interference with their economic activities, rooting out of command and administrative methods of economic management and broad utilization of economic levers and incentives.

4. Implementation of deep structural economic transformations which secure the effective utilization of material, natural and labour resources, manufacture of competitive output and integration into the world economic system.

5. Formation of a new economic mentality of the people, alteration of their world outlook, provision of an opportunity for every individual to independently determine spheres and forms of application of their labour.

Moreover, it is to be kept in mind that any reform makes sense when it meets the interests of a man and promotes satisfaction of his or her needs and requirements and when it is directed towards raising the well-being of the people.

Consistent achievement of strategic objectives predetermined the need to clearly identify major priorities of the first stage of reform. Moreover, it was vitally important to find out those principal links which could be utilized to solve the most acute problems within the feasible future.

Our entire programme of market transformations is built on the stage-by-stage solution of tasks of prior significance.

The first stage — the initial link in the chain of moves on transition from totalitarian past to modern, civilized market relations — constitutes the specific and complex features of the current period.

Two decisive tasks had to be solved simultaneously at the first stage:

— **get over painful consequences of the administrative-command system, overcome the crisis and stabilize the economy;**

— **shape the fundamentals of market relations with consideration of the country's specific peculiarities and conditions.**

Solution of these tasks at the first stage required the singling out of the following major priorities which determined basic guidelines of initial economic reform.

First, the formation of legal foundations of the transition process, consolidation and development of a legislative and legal basis of reform. The adoption of a Fundamental Law — new Constitution of the Republic of Uzbekistan, a legal foundation of state independence and contemporary economic relations,— was raised to the level of the main task.

Second, setting up the basis of a multi-structural economy on account of shaping new forms of ownership in rural economy, implementation of privatization and decentralization of the enterprises of local industries, trade, public amenities services, housing stock, as well as establishment of joint-stock companies at the enterprises of the light industry, civil engineering and transport.

Creation of favourable conditions for the development of private businesses, ensuring constitutional rights and guarantees for the protection of private proprietorship. Re-establishment of genuinely cooperative forms of production in the country-side on account of reorganization of state farms into collective farms or other non-state forms of ownership, development of dekhkan (peasant) farms, small cooperative, contractor and household leasing farms.

Third, a major condition for the realization of economic reform is getting over the further production decline and securing stabilization of financial situation.

Successful transition to market is possible solely on condition of stable operation of economy. The situation which took shape at the first stage required the adoption of operative, tough, sometimes unpopular measures to overcome the crisis and prevent rapid deterioration of the living standard of the population.

Major and top-priority moves advanced at the first stage included:

In the Field of Financial and Tax Policies:

— tough financial policy, reduction of state budget deficit to permissible minimal limit and gradual reduction of all budget subsidies;

— persistent implementation of the course which presupposed the assignment of budgetary means only after the receipt of revenues and assignment of budgetary means only to the most urgent and top-priority needs of the state;

— denial of gratuitous financing of branches of national economy and separate enterprises on account of state budget and broad utilization of investment loans for these purposes;

— further improvement of the tax system, implementation of flexible tax policy ensuring stable inflow of revenues into the budget, stimulating the development of small private businesses, joint ventures with foreign capital for processing farm produce and for the manufacture of consumer commodities;

In the Field of Credit and Monetary Policies:

— formation of two-level bank system headed by the Central Bank and a broad network of independent commercial and private banks, creation of favourable conditions for opening branches and representations of major foreign banks;

— ensuring stable currency circulation, radical limitation of emission of credit and cash and overall growth of money supply;

— creation of necessary economic and organizational conditions and prerequisites for the introduction into circulation of a national monetary unit of the Republic of Uzbekistan;

In the Field of Price and Anti-Inflation Policies:

— further regulation of the price-formation system and consolidation of the role of pricing as a market regulator;

— obvious recognition of unacceptability of "shocking" price liberalization mechanism for Uzbekistan and subsequent realization of stage-by-stage liberalization of wholesale and retail prices with gradual expansion of the list of commodities sold at free (contracted) prices;

— temporary preservation of state price regulation only on a limited range of vital food products, first of all, on flour and bread;

— consistent raising of procurement prices on farm produce with bringing them up to the level of world prices;

— implementation of measures on prevention of artificial price-rise on account of carrying out anti-monopoly moves, breaking up highly-monopolistic structures into smaller units and creation of competitive environment.

One of the most strategically important priorities realized during the entire reform was the implementation of structural transformations. To ensure strategic growth means to change the structure of production. Hence, depending upon available resources at each stage, concrete measures should be elaborated on structural changes, primarily in the top-priority sectors of economy.

Major stress at the first stage was made on:

— a deeper processing of principal farm crops (cotton, silk, fruit and vegetables and other products), development of associated productions in the light and local industries —textile, weaving, knitting, garment-making, etc.;

— accelerated development of branches manufacturing major types of consumer commodities, manufacture of broader range of goods, establishment of new production lines on the output of table salt, alcohol, matches and such other goods in great demand;

— the implementation of measures on lessening dependency of the Republic on the import from other regions of manufactured goods and commodities vitally important for the needs of national economy and the population on the basis of development of competitive productions;

— ensuring advanced development of fuel and power complex, increasing the volume of extraction and processing of oil and natural gas with the aim of achieving power independence of the country.

Agricultural reform is identified as a key link in the implementation of economic transformations.

Problems of development of the agrarian sector of economy have been decisive in the entire strategy of Uzbekistan's transition to market relations. Hence, rural economy is going to be constantly in the centre of reform in progress, since it is the basis of our whole economy. We have admitted more than once that the impact of radical transformations and reform on the rural sector and the villages, to a great extent, determine the outcome of all economic transformations.

Major tasks in the field of reformation of rural economy at the first stage included:

— broad development of new forms of farming and management in the country-side, the formation of such economic relations which enable farmers to feel themselves genuine masters of the land they toil and the output they produce;

— consistent implementation of the policy which provides for turning plantations under cotton and other farm crops for the organization of dekhkan (peasant) farms, expansion of personal plots and allotment of farm land to rural residents for perpetual use with the right to inherit;

— implementation of deep progressive moves in the agricultural sphere aimed at optimization of the structure of lands under crops, reducing the share of cotton, increasing the output of food products, primarily, the output of grain crops;

— maximum possible location of processing industries to sources of agricultural raw, establishment of small compact industrial enterprises and businesses, broad stimulation of craftsmen working at home and development of a network of businesses for servicing the needs of agricultural production;

— active formation of a broad network of social and production infrastructure in the rural areas and secure supply of rural settlements with running water and natural gas.

An important link in the stabilization of economy is a reliable supply of population with food products. This is one of the fundamental priorities of the republic's agricultural policy. The achievement of genuine economic independence requires the solution of the fundamental problem of food supply. Raising the level of self-supply of grain, potato, live-stock produce, sugar and other food products is the immediate task facing the country.

The all-round development and efficient utilization of the republic's export potential grows into the most vital condition of strengthening the economy. For decades our country has actually been isolated from the outside world. The principal objective of the first stage was to establish ourselves in the world community, confirm the image of a reliable partner and develop extensive external economic ties, which required:

— setting up specialized organizational structures on the implementation of foreign political and external economic activities and organization of training of corresponding personnel;

— conducting a policy aimed at the liberalization of external economic activity, providing greater freedom to enterprises and citizens for the establishment of direct relations with foreign partners;

— introduction of benefits for the export and import of goods, gradual shortening of the list of commodities subject to quoting and licensing;

— further improvement of the export and import structure. Expansion of deliveries of finished, technically sophisticated goods and commodities to foreign countries, rendering transportation, tourist and currency-credit services along with the export of traditional produce (cotton, cotton products, non-ferrous metals, mineral fertilizer, etc.);

— stimulation of investment activities of enterprises in the sphere of export-oriented output through introduction of a system of benefits, establishment of joint ventures and securing the protection of foreign investors rights and interests;

— immediate channelling of foreign loans for the delivery of the most vital food products and medicine, attracting foreign investments to basic sectors of national economy — mining, fuel and energy, industrial processing of farm produce and to the development of non-state sector of economy;

— establishment of the infrastructure of external economic activity — specialized foreign trade, leasing, consulting and insurance companies, a system of transport and communications which meets the interests and corresponds to conditions of development of external relations and opening of representations abroad.

Along with the aforesaid fundamental priorities of our programme of economic reform there are a number of stand out priorities which need to be clearly identified and which retain their priority at all stages of the reform. They run through all trends and directions of the process of society renovation.

These priorities ensure the succession of all stages of the reform and its continuous nature, create conditions for making transformations irreversible.

A stand out priority in the implementation of the reform strategy means for us the realization of strong measures on social protection of the population, the most important among them are the following:

— ensurng reliable guarantees for socio-political stability, civil peace and inter-ethnic accord in the Republic;

— further consolidation of the principles of social justice, establishment of an effective mechanism for social protection of the most needy strata of the population — the aged, disabled, orphans, families with many children and students;

— ensuring that social assistance purposefully reaches those to whom it is addressed to, raises its efficiency on account of unifying the system of benefits and other allowances in direct connection with real incomes of the population;

— raising the role of self-administration agencies of citizens, makhallya (neighbourhood) committees in the solution of problems of social protection of the most vulnerable sections of the population through creation of conditions for activization of specialized foundations for social maintenance of people with low-income;

— regulation of the labour market and conducting an active employment policy, stimulation of conditions for creating new job opportunities in areas with excess labour force on account of development of small and medium businesses.

Other stand out priorities include the development and reformation of education and culture, consolidation of intellectual and spiritual potentials.

The economic reform may succeed only on condition that our nation will be able to truly realize its freedom and, the spirit, customs and traditions of our forefathers will be revived. Only highly educated, firm and spiritually strong people can manage to go along the road of renovation and progress. Spirituality of our nation, going back to ideas and aspirations of our great ancestors, serves as a solid and powerful foundation for our economic transformations.

1.2. ESTABLISHMENT OF A LEGAL BASIS IS AN IMPORTANT RESULT OF THE FIRST STAGE OF ECONOMIC REFORM

One of the basic factors in the implementation of economic reform is the establishment of legal basis of a market economy. From the very outset we derived a major lesson for ourselves: without forming the necessary legal foundation and without passing corresponding laws and normative acts there can be no talk about practical guarantees for the implementation of reform, the guarantee that the reform would not fall backwards.

Only a solid legal foundation may ensure full confidence in the possibility of reconstruction of the old obsolete system and **building a new society with civilized market economy.** It is namely a code of new laws which reflect principally new modern political, economic and legal relations and serve as a framework that provides stability and democratic feature to our entire newly-established social structure. That is to say, these laws, oriented to ensuring the interests of the republic's population and protecting its rights and liberties, create strong social motivation for radical transformations and instill confidence in the bright future of Uzbekistan.

Hence the most important element which we laid stress on at the first stage was the establishment of our own legal basis of reform.

A number of circumstances predetermined the need for the elaboration and adoption of a whole package of new laws.

First, the laws in force served the interests of protecting the past totalitarian regime. The previous legislation had imposed norms consolidating the administrative-command principle of economic management, recognizing solely state ownership of the means of production and fully excluding the right of private ownership, free competition and limiting the effect of the law of value.

Pseudo-socialist principles introduced norms of imaginary social justice, which actually recognized egalitarianism engendering dependency, social and labour apathy and economic irresponsibility.

All legal acts related to economic life were imbued with a spirit of a centralized planning system of organization of national economy, where there was practically no space either for economic freedom of enterprises or economic initiative or entrepreneurship.

The economy and its legal foundation had been ideologized for decades and ignored the requirements of international norms and rules. In legal respect we had been confined within the limits of the socialist camp and actually had no access to the world community as an equal entity of international law.

To put it short the entire legal foundation serves as the main obstacle for shaping new economic relations. From the very start of reform all our moves came in conflict with the legislation and normative acts then in force. Thus to be able to ensure the advancement of reform we had first to bring our whole legislative system into line with new conditions and new objectives.

Second, all legal acts adopted in Uzbekistan in the past were fully adapted to All-Union norms and never took into account the specific regional peculiarities of our Republic.

The right to initiate legislation rested with the Moscow Kremlin. Republican legislative organs merely copied laws, party or Government resolutions adopted at the Union level. The majority of resolutions were eclectic in their essence, cut off from real conditions and sometimes contradicted national peculiarities, traditions and interests of the Republic and encroached upon its sovereignty. As a result, serious disproportions and exaggerations took shape in the economy and socio-spiritual spheres requiring their soonest possible elimination.

After gaining its independence Uzbekistan, as a newly-proclaimed state faced the task of elaborating and adopting a new legal foundation meeting the interests of the nation and the tasks of democratic transformations both of society and economic relations.

And, **third**, we have chosen our own road of renovation and progress, our own model for reforming the economy and hence, the use of legal norms and acts of other countries, however market-oriented they might be, was not acceptable for us. We have thoroughly examined and studied the experiences of making laws in many countries of the world with established democratic norms and principles of market economy. This enabled us to avoid mistakes and within the shortest terms form a solid modern legal basis, elaborate our own mechanism for legal protection of reform with consideration of specifics of building a reformed society. Quite a number of adopted laws have been preliminarily considered by experts of well-known international law agencies and have been highly evaluated for their legal maturity and correspondence to generally-accepted norms and rules.

At the first stage we elaborated our own approaches to the creation of legal foundations, our own mechanism for the elaboration and adoption of legal acts. We have drawn an important conclusion for ourselves: it is vital to learn to administer the society through laws. Law should become the chief regulator of social life and public relations. For this need thoroughly elaborated and comprehensively substantiated laws of long duration.

Currently, we have shaped an integral system of state and legal regulation of the reform process. It organically combines all structures of power: presidential form of government, legislative, executive and judicial ones. Moreover, it firmly leans on the principles of glasnost, openness and broad discussion of resolutions expected to be adopted.

The basic strategic principles in the field of state structure and economic reform are initiated and approved by Decrees issued by the President of the Republic of Uzbekistan. Namely these Decrees reflect the main ideology and primal landmarks in the implementation of the policy of reform. Namely these Decrees reveal the purposeful nature of radical resolutions and mechanism of their realization.

Fundamental norms and provisions with stable and durable effect find their reflection in Laws. Legally consolidated norms acquire are mandatory for direct observance for all economic entities irrespective of their form of proprietorship. With the advancement and deepening of reform, its legal basis is being further improved and perfected and necessary corrections and amendments are being timely introduced into legal acts currently in force. This enables to raise the efficiency of laws, directly tie them up to shaping socio-economic conditions.

Resolutions adopted in Decrees are revealed in detail on the legal foundation and consolidated by concrete measures in the Government resolutions. The process of operative state and legal regulation of economic reform's advancement and transformations of major sectors and spheres of economy are implemented through adoption of Government resolutions.

The moves undertaken at the government level are subordinated to the solution of major national economic problems and clearly direct all participants in the reform process towards its key aspects. Many a resolution, in their content and in outlining problems, bear a defining nature, serving as a starting point for the expansion of reform in certain sectors of economy. A number of crucial resolutions adopted in 1994 alone opened up principally new approaches to the solution of the problems of consolidation of national currency, reduction of currency emission, filling the republican consumer market with marketable goods, currency regulation, deepening economic reform in rural economy and development of dekhkan (peasant) farms, improvement of the structure of industrial management, etc.

Considering Laws, Decrees and Resolutions in their unity and interrelation there is every ground to state that we managed to form an integral, progressive system of state-legal guarantees of reform in progress.

The very system of making laws and mechanism of elaboration and adoption of legal and normative acts has been formed in this country in recent years. The principle of open and broad discussion of drafts of major documents advanced for approval has firmly established itself in practice. All legal and normative acts intended for approval are published in the press, covered over the television and other means of mass media for consideration of the broadest strata of the population. Active explanatory campaign with the participation of the members of Government, MPs, scientists and specialists is carried out to bring the most vital issues and provisions to the attention of the public.

A special Inter-Departmental Council on economic reform, entrepreneurship and foreign investments has been set up under the President of the Republic of Uzbekistan for the purpose of collective discussion and adoption of resolutions of the most important problems of exceptional significance for the further accelerated implementation of reform. Major objectives and directions of the Council's activity include elaboration of a unified strategy of socio-economic development and practical moves for its realization, preparation of recommendations on the improvement of economic reform's legal basis, elaboration of concrete models and programmes of economic transformations in the Republic, analysis of conditions for the development of entrepreneurship, defining a system of measures on active attraction of foreign investments.

In the course of its activity the Council discussed in detail such problems as basic guidelines, principles and mechanisms of further deepening the privatization of state property, forming the securities market and organization of stock exchange activity, measures on securing stability of national currency, stimulation of development of activity, initiation and stimulation of development of private ownership and adopted recommendations, which formed the basis for Decrees issued by the President of the Republic of Uzbekistan. The Council has provided thorough analysis and evaluated the course of execution of Government resolutions on further advancement of economic reform in rural economy. Questions advanced for the consideration of the Council are discussed openly, in a principled and constructive manner. This enables, when adopting decisions, to more fully take account of a broad spectrum of specialists views and recommendations.

Much has already been accomplished in legal respect on the road of building market relations. Legal institutions and code of laws are being established consistently, which ensures the implementation of market relations in a civilized form. About 100 basic legal acts related to the sphere of economy, establishing the legal basis for reforming economic relations, have been currently adopted in this country. Legal basis of reform has been introduced along several major directions.

The first direction — establishment of legal foundation of state and economic independence of Uzbekistan, creation of new laws regulating the principles of state administration. Such historical laws as the Law "On the Fundamentals of State Independence of the Republic of Uzbekistan", Laws "On Mineral Resources", "On the Cabinet of Ministers of the Republic of Uzbekistan", "On Local Government Administration", "On Organs of Self-Administration by Citizens", etc. have been passed to match these trends.

As a result of adopted laws it has been recognized that land, natural and mineral resources and production potential are an inalienable and exceptional property of the people of Uzbekistan.

The functions of administrative structures at the national and local levels have been clearly identified. The institute of khokims (Governors and Mayors), meeting best national conditions, was introduced in the country as the sole full-blooded organ of representative power in provinces. A unique mechanism of self-administration, rooted back in national traditions and historically formed communal relations — makhallya (neighbourhood) has taken shape in Uzbekistan. The assembly of residents of settlements, villages and neighbourhoods has been recognized as the organ of self-administrastion providing citizens with their right to participate in the administration of state affairs and uniting them for the solution of social and economic tasks in their respective territories.

The second direction — formation of a code of laws laying the foundation of systematic transformations, qualitatively new economic relations and, first and foremost, relations of ownership. Among these basic, fundamental laws, adopted by the Supreme Council of the Republic are the laws on ownership, on land, on decentralization and privatization, on lease, on privatization of state housing stock, etc.

The right of ownership forms the basis of economic transformations. The right of an owner is recognized and protected by law in the Republic. Uzbekistan was one of the first to recognize the right of private ownership and created equal conditions for all forms of ownership. Juridical and organizational prerequisites have been created, and effective mechanism of privatization of state property and transformation of state enterprises into other forms of proprietorship have been practically elaborated and approved.

Attitude concerning the problem of ownership of land has been legally defined without any option. On the basis of specifics of irrigated farming, historical peculiarities of land and water use in Uzbekistan, it was determined that land can be turned over to those who toil it with the right to use and inherit it.

Eventually all legal conditions opening up possibilities for the formation of multi-structural economy, as an essential condition and basis of market relations, have been created in this country today.

The third and most dynamically developing direction of making laws — creation of frame conditions for a new mechanism of economic management and institutional transformations. This theme is represented by a large package of laws and normative acts regulating all aspects of enterprises and organizations economic activities and ensuring the formation of a new market infrastructure.

To begin with, laws determining the status, rights and economic freedoms of economic entities in various spheres of economy were adopted; among them are laws on enterprises, on cooperation, on dekhkan farms, on economic societies and partnerships. These laws contained for the first time the fundamental principles of new economic mechanism in the Republic on the basis of economic incentive, profit-making and material responsibility for the results of economic activity.

Introduction of these laws diversified the organizational and legal forms of enterprises (collective, share-holding, societies with limited responsibility, cooperatives, partnerships, joint ventures, etc.). These forms correspond to the greatest extent to enterprises activities and system of their management under new conditions.

Legislative norms regulating processes of establishment and operation of market infrastructure were actively shaped and implemented. Their basic clauses find their expression in the laws on banks and banking activity, on monetary system, on entrepreneurship, on insurance, on exchange and exchange operations, on auditing, on securities and equities, on stock exchange, etc. The adoption of these laws laid strong foundation for the development of market mechanisms in the Republic.

Vital significance within the system of state regulation of shaping market relations belongs to the adoption of legal acts determining the mechanism of inter-relations between economically independent enterprises and citizens with the state through the system of taxes, limitation of monopolistic activities, introduction of mortgage right and official recognition of enterprises bankruptcy. All arising disputes will have to be solved now by civilized methods through courts. With this goal in sight an economic procedural code of the Republic of Uzbekistan has been elaborated and economic arbitration has been set up.

Despite the adoption of numerous legal acts the process of shaping a new economic law has not yet been completed. This trend in making laws is expected to retain its dynamic nature at subsequent stages of reform. A Civil Code will have to be adopted within feasible future, which will reflect all major legal provisions regulating the economic activity of all forms of ownership.

The fourth direction — creation of legal norms, identifying Uzbekistan as an equal entity of international relations. The laws adopted in relation to external economic ties, on Uzbekistan's membership in leading international organizations, on currency regulation, signing of major international pacts and agreements by Uzbekistan have opened up a qualitatively new page in the history of our country's external relations.

Of particular significance for Uzbekistan are fundamental principles for broad attraction of investments into our economy and providing reliable rights and guarantees of protection of foreign investors interests. Foreign investments are not merely a living link with the outside world, but also are a source of deep structural and systematic transformations without which there can be no talk about building a renewed society.

The fifth and the most important direction — elaboration of legislation ensuring the observation of reliable constitutional and juridical human rights, social guarantees and social support of the population. Preparation, discussion and adoption of fundamental laws regulating and providing guarantees of human rights and freedoms, rights and freedoms of public organizations and freedom of conscience and religion have been something principally new in practical law making in this country.

Adopted laws on employment, on social protection of disabled, on entitlement of citizens to state pension, on education, on fundamentals of state policy in regard to the youth, and on freedom of conscience and religious organizations provided an opportunity to protect by force of law the interests of the most vulnerable strata of the population in complicated conditions of transition to market relations, and to reveal spiritual and creative potential of the people and placed a solid social foundation for reform.

The law making activity at the first stage was crowned with adoption of the first Constitution — the Fundamental Law of the state and social life — of independent Uzbekistan. The Constitution serves as a solid foundation of genuine independence of our newly-established state engendering new social and economic relations.

The fundamental principles of state and economic reform, expounded and practically implemented in Decrees and Laws of the Republic of Uzbekistan establish a solid legal basis for transition period, for the period of legal replacement of outlived economic relations and the political system and for assertion of truly democratic norms and social guarantees.

The objective at the first stage was not only to elaborate and pass laws, adequate to contemporary conditions, but also secure their stringent observation. It was also urgent to elaborate such a mode of legislation, such level of juridical education and culture, under which the observation of law becomes a must for all, and its violation — simply inadmissible by everybody.

Successful implementation of all normative and legal acts is closely associated with bringing up a new conscience and juridical culture in comprehension of law. It is everybody's secret that the level of legal culture is determined by the execution of adopted laws, not by their quantity. The road to market economy will have to become a school of legal education for us. An important lesson to remember is that, we will have to learn to live and work in compliance with law, learn to protect our rights and freedoms by law and strictly fulfil our obligations. We will have to learn to be respectful about rights, freedoms and interests of other people. We should strive to ensure a triumph of the power of law, while its strict observation should grow in every one of us into sacred responsibility and obligation.

1.3. PRIVATIZATION OF STATE PROPERTY AND SHAPING OF MULTI-STRUCTURAL ECONOMY

A fundamental condition of transition to market relations is creation of legal and organizational prerequisites for shaping a multi-structural economy and competitive environment.

A corner-stone of the entire system of measures on shaping market economy is the solution of the problem of ownership. It plays the most significant role and is most acute namely in the post-socialist countries, which have taken to the road of market transformations. That is to say, the solution of this problem lays the first stone into the foundation of a new society and new economic relations. Namely differences in the solution of the problem of ownership chosen by newly independent states explain variance of approaches and models of transformation of planned centralized economy into market relations. Successful solution of this problem in compliance with demands of the time is the principal factor called upon to place our Republic into the ranks of advanced industrial countries of the world.

Equality of all forms of ownership was recognized constitutionally at the first stage reform in Uzbekistan. Equitable legal norms and mechanisms of application have been established for their efficient making. Moreover, there is a whole system of tax benefits and preferences stimulating dynamic development of newly-organized or privatized enterprises based on private ownership or with the participation of foreign capital. Thus, practically all legal and organizational obstacles have been removed today which previously artificially restricted the development of non-governmental private sector and entrepreneurship.

An exceptional peculiarity of shaping a multi-structural economy in post-socialist countries, Uzbekistan included, and differing in principle from the countries where the making of market economy advanced in an evolutionary way is that the formation of a non-government sector is carried out mostly on account of denationalization and privatization of state property.

Privatization of state property is effected also in economically advanced countries, such as Great Britain, France, Japan, the Philippines, etc. This is a natural process of development of market relations, particularly in countries with sufficiently high share of state sector of economy. The state is called upon to maintain and take care about financing and rendering support to individual sectors of economy and individual enterprises which more often than not are economically inefficient, but play a major role in a country's general economic development. With their gradual economic consolidation and stable operation, they are subject for sale to private owners.

This is not the case in the former socialist countries which carry out economic reforms. Before regaining their independence, private ownership of the means of production was completely neglected. It used to be the first indication and difference between capitalist and socialist methods of production. Hence followed that private ownership was excluded both de jure and practically de facto. Only its modified form "called personal property of citizens" had the right to existence and it was not considered the means of production and could not produce any kind of profit. All types of income made by the people from the use of their property was considered illegal.

For decades the state sector fully dominated the economy in the form of a so-called nation-wide ownership, though eventually it was fully controlled by the state bureaucratic system. The entire diversity of the forms of ownership was reduced down to two of its types: state and collective-farm/cooperative ownership. Moreover, the latter was actually also fully centralized.

Thus all means of production used to be monopolistic property of the state. This resulted in tearing away of direct participants in production from the means of production and in losing the sense of proprietorship and any economic interest in stimulation of labour. Only an economically independent citizen, a genuine proprietor can be deeply interested in the efficient utilization of his property to multiply both his own wealth and enrich his country.

Therefore, the most crucial task of the first stage of economic reform was to abolish the monopoly of state ownership and practically form a multi-structural economy on account of its privatization.

Many countries which go through the process of privatization have accumulated their own experience and elaborated their own approaches to transformation of the forms of ownership. In principle they differ in their objectives of privatization, dynamics and mechanism of implementation of this process and degree of population's involvement in privatization processes.

Thus in Russia, the objective of mass privatization was to form within the shortest possible period a broad stratum of proprietors on account of setting up joint-stock companies at all state enterprises and establishment of securities / voucher market. Moreover, privatization was not considered as a factor for ensuring economic and financial stability. As a result, a stratum of genuine, economically viable proprietors has so far failed to be formed on the background of broad privatization symbolizing a process of rapid advance towards market relations. On the contrary, this process was accompanied by production decline and greater financial disbalance, while many enterprises, which changed their form of ownership, went bankrupt and resold for a song. Instead of broad stratum of proprietors, holders of vouchers, a broad network of financial and holding companies and voucher funds emerged which collected their capital on account of economic illiteracy of the people. This furthered social stratification of the society.

With consideration of the experience of our own model of transition to market economy we have elaborated and practically tested some principled approaches to privatization and formation of Uzbekistan's multi-structural economy. What are they?

In the first place, we rejected from the very beginning the idea of voucher privatization, although some foreign experts had been very insistent to impose it on us. The idea was unacceptable for a number of reasons however attractive it could look with a stress on ensuring the principle of social justice.

First, it is hardly possible to objectively determine each resident's contribution to the production potential of the country, which was created by the efforts of several generations. To estimate the value of property, issue cheques or vouchers or whatever securities to this value, and then distribute equally among all residents of the country does not mean observation of the principle of social justice; this again looks like a distorted form of faceless socialist all-levelling.

Second, free distribution of bonds with subsequent purchase of enterprises shares does not set up an army of proprietors, on the contrary, it devaluates our wealth. If received for gratis any property or part of it, it cannot be expected to be valued or efficiently utilized, as is the case when it was bought for one's hard-earned money. **No price — no value.** We have learnt well this bitter lesson. It is not a mere coincidence that many "new Russians" watch indifferently the collapse of enterprises, the shares of which they hold, or how various joint-stock and investment funds burst with sensation and scandal like soap-bubbles.

We have arrived at a definite conclusion that **state property may be transformed into other form of ownership only through its sale to a new proprietor** — with the exception of projects of social infrastructure and ecology. The essence of such approach to decentralization and privatization was rather simple: to abandon a faceless "voucherized" proprietor and turn over property to a proprietor capable to use the property he/she received and ensure its efficient utilization already at the first stage of his/her activity. This approach fully justifies itself. Instead of expected production decline and bankruptcies, as the case is in a number of other countries, the majority of privatized enterprises in this country display higher productivity and themselves manage to break through the hardships of transition period.

Receipts from privatization are channelled, first and foremost, to support these same enterprises during the post-privatization period, for the establishment of new competitive businesses, which is not the least of the factors. This is a considerable relief for the budget and provides an opportunity to accumulate free investment resources and concentrate them on reform's top-priority trends.

Third, the efficient operation of the bond market presupposes a high level ability of dealing with securities and equities, operability of a corresponding structure and a system of guarantees. Lack of experience in dealing with securities, lack of clear understanding about which sectors or enterprises deserve best to be invested in, as well as the fact that the majority of the population is involved in agricultural production mean that the introduction of bond privatization would inevitably deteriorate the social situation. And this is something which fully runs counter against the principles of reform we have chosen.

The second specific peculiarity is the ensurance of a programmed approach and stage-by-stage implementation of privatization. The Law On Decentralization and Privatization clearly states that all activity on transformation of the forms of ownership is effected stage-by-stage — on the basis of special programmes elaborated and approved at the national and territorial levels.

Such approach enabled us to identify major priorities in the field of privatization for each stage. At the initial stage the privatization process covered public housing, enterprises of trade, local industries and the sphere of services and organizations dealing with the procurement of farm produce — the so-called "privatization minor". Individual medium and large enterprises of the light and local industries, transport and civil engineering and other industries, were transformed, as a rule, into leasing enterprises with the right of their subsequent redemption; collective enterprises and closed type joint-stock companies where the state retains the control package of shares. At this stage in the course of privatization proper, the mechanisms of decentralization and denationalization was being adjusted, and popular mentality changed in favour of decentralization.

Greater experience further advanced the process of privatization, which received a qualitatively new impetus following the Decree of January 21, 1994 on measures on deepening economic reform and the Decree of March 16, 1994 on top-priority guidelines of further development of decentralization and privatization. In compliance with the adopted resolutions, the main task put forward at this stage was to expand the process of setting up joint-stock companies of an open type through transformation of enterprises while drawing in to this process the population and foreign investors. It was envisaged to radically reduce the share of state on account of broadening the number of participants. A foundation was laid for shaping the securities and real estate market; auctions and sales of state property started to be held on a regular basis.

Privatization is carried out on a consistent and systematic basis. More than 20 state programmes on decentralization and privatization have been adopted and are being implemented in various sectors of economy and provinces of the Republic.

The following specific peculiarity of the approach to privatization is that we have established and maintain strong social guarantees for the population in the course of decentralization. Moreover, the principle of equality of citizens for getting a share of property is strictly adhered to, as well as social protection of members of a privatized enterprise's personnel.

Social guarantee primarily means that privatization includes a whole system of benefits. Thus, personnel of a privatized enterprise enjoys the right to purchase shares on favourable terms. Fixed assets with a high degree of depreciation and projects of social infrastructure are turned over to a new proprietor for gratis. Privatization of state farms, farms, gardens and vineyards is carried out on preferential terms. A discount from redemption value of property envisaged in case a privatized enterprise purchased fixed assets on account of its own resources from production development fund. Many trade and service enterprises have been sold to their new proprietors along with plots of land. With the view of rendering post-privatization support for those enterprises they also enjoy some tax benefits.

Thus, the system of social guarantees is called upon to create maximum favourable conditions both for the implementation of privatization and for their successful post-privatization start-up and operation.

Another specific feature of our privatization mechanism, along with a change of ownership and breaking up of enterprises into smaller units, is the demonopolization of long-established production and administrative structures. This was particularly well displayed in the branches of the light and local industries and in agro-industrial complex. Not only new proprietors sprang up, but there emerged a real competitive environment.

What are the concrete results we have been able to achieve at the first stage of economic reform in the field of privatization and development of entrepreneurship?

The main result is a practical completion of "privatization minor", the establishment of institutional structures and special agencies designed to manage state property and its transformation into other forms of ownership.

At the first stage, this process of privatization was most dynamically implemented in the sphere of "privatization minor" carried out mainly on the basis of turning over the enterprises of trade, public amenities services and the local industries for private and collective (cooperative) ownership. It was already completed back in 1994 and currently (early 1995) more than 82 per cent of gross output of trade and public catering fall on the non-state sector. In accordance with privatization programmes adopted by the sub-divisions of the "Mahalliy Sanoat" (Local Industries) Corporation, the overwhelming majority of enterprises of "Uzbeksavdo" (Association of Trade Enterprises), "Uzbekbirlashu" (Consumer Cooperative Society of Uzbekistan) and Uzbytsoyuz (Association of Public Amenities Services) have been transformed into other forms of ownership.

The experiences of privatized trade and public service enterprises prove that their new proprietors managed to raise dramatically the level of services, expanded the choice of goods and services and capital, and routine repairs were carried out at every one of their establishments.

Privatization of housing was the initial step. More than one million apartments earlier controlled by the state or 95 per cent of state housing stock have been turned into personal property of citizens in the course of privatization. Moreover, every third apartment was turned over to their residents either on favourable terms or for free. Veterans of war, teachers, medical personnel, scientists and creative intelligentcia paid nothing to become the owners of their flats.

For disabled and single aged persons with low income, for newly-weds and other socially vulnerable categories of citizens in need of housing, local administrations set up special communal housing funds intended to be let on the basis of agreements without the right to privatize.

Enterprises and organizations have the right to fully or partially repay loans or credits for housing construction or privatization of apartments to its personnel and pensioners.

With the privatization of housing stock, the system of communal services underwent a radical transformation. It's now full control of local administrations. Provinces are more independent now and subsequently bear greater responsibility for rendering communal services to the population. This sector was turned over to local Councils not merely nominally but through financially.

The implementation of "privatization minor" and accumulation of corresponding experience in the administrative and economic management structures enabled from mid - 1994 onward to start the stage of privatization en masse directed towards the establishment of the open-type share-holding societies; issuance of enterprises shares setting up wide-scale real estate and securities markets, and thereafter proceed with decentralization and privatization of medium-size and big industrial, civil engineering and transport enterprises, the enterprises of the meat and dairy, food and cotton-ginning industries of agroindustrial complex. Considerable attention is attached to privatization of tourist complexes in Tashkent, Bukhara, Samarkand and Khiva.

The very mechanism of privatization underwent further improvement in the course of the first stage. The scheme of formation of open type share-holding societies under major state enterprises was brought to further perfection by practice. Share-holding societies may be founded in the first place by the staff of an enterprise and foreign investors prepared to invest resources into technical re-equipment of production; or the state; which also envisages free floating of shares through stock exchanges, even abroad. Meanwhile, it clearly defines that the portion of shares which belong to the state should sharply decrease. Currently it cannot exceed 26 per cent. More than half of the package of shares is subject to free realization.

With the purpose of speeding up reform in the country-side, a programme of decentralization and development of multi-structural economy in the agriculture has been elaborated and implemented in Uzbekistan. A concept of economic development of a district was elaborated for the Tashkent rural district which will serve the basis for working out the guidelines of deepening economic reform at the district level.

New forms of decentralization of state property, through open sales and at auctions, are being widely practiced within the system of privatization moves. The results of the first sales indicate that this form is quite a promising one and an ever-greater number of new proprietors wish to take part in them. Objects of trade and the sphere of services — shops, restaurants, hotels, etc.— as a rule, are sold currently at auctions. What is more, actual value of sold property by far exceeds its starting price. This provides an opportunity to most realistically appraise the value of privatized property and contributes to the consolidation of our national currency.

A new form of auctions has recently become popular — apart from property, plots of land under privatized trade abd public services ebterprises are set out for auction, and the owners, including foreign investors, have the right to use this land for new construction. Transfers of farm land in perpetual use with the right to inherit are organized at auctions and sales.

Institutional structures of real estate and securities markets was recently initiated in this country. The Republican stock exchange, National depository and investment funds have been set and a programme of establishing an information-telecommunication system elaborated in Uzbekistan.

The Republican stock exchange, which opened its brokers offices in the provinces, holds regular sales to draw the broad public into the process of privatization and accelerate the formation of securities market.

The real estate market too takes its shape. Among sold projects, dominate apartment houses, trade and public service enterprises and construction in progress. And this is only the beginning.

The process of decentralization and privatization is gaining momentum. About 54 thousand enterprises and projects had been decentralized from the beginning of privatization of state property untill the end of 1994. Among them 18.4 thousand are currently privately owned, 26.1 are owned by share-holding companies, 8.7 thousand are in collective ownership and 661 are leased enterprises. Joint ventures with the participation of foreign capital are established on the basis of privatized enterprises. Two out of three enterprises today are in the form of non-state ownership. In 1994 almost half of the GNP was manufactured in the non-state sector of economy.

Loans to enterprises in the post-privatization period for realization of concrete projects on technical re-equipment and restructuring of production are issued on account of resources received from decentralization and privatization of enterprises. This provides an opportunity to support private entrepreneurs, mostly farmers, with loans and credits.

An impetus was given to the development of small businesses. The number of small business enterprises doubled in recent years. A fund for the development of entrepreneurship and a fund for the promotion of small and medium businesses have been established in this country to render support to the non-state sector.

All these moves aimed at rendering assistance to the development of private sector provided an opportunity to bring the number of private enterprises up to almost 20 thousand by the early 1995. More than 250 thousand people are engaged in individual labour. And about 4.0 million people are employed in the non-state sector of economy, which constitutes almost half of all employed in social production. This is a vivid proof of actual advancement toward market economy.

Taking active part in the processes of decentralization and privatization are a number of international organizations, among them UNIDO which helped establish three business-incubators. The Commission of European Community organized a Business Relations Centre. The German Society of Technical Assistance founded a Centre for Promotion of small and medium businesses. The American Business Foundation and British Central Asian Investment Fund are active in Central Asia and render broad consultative services and help organize training of personnel.

The effect of privatization is of dual nature — on the one hand, it attracts free resources of the population and thus reduces their pressure on the market, but simultaneously creates conditions for drawing in new sources into production and promotes competition among manufacturers. At the same time, this process increases the income of the population on account of efficient operation of privatized enterprises.

However significant are the visible achievements in shaping a modern multi-structural economy, we arrive at an inevitable conclusion that the process of privatization has merely started its broad offensive. Its further deepening should play a major role in the implementation of subsequent stages of economic reform.

1.4. REFORMATION OF AGRICULTURE AND FORMATION OF AGRARIAN RELATIONS OF A NEW TYPE

At the first stage of implementation of economic reforms, particular priority was attached to reformation of rural economy in Uzbekistan. This is explained by the role played by agriculture and those sectors associated with processing of agricultural raw materials in the economy of our country.

The share of agrarian sector by January 1, 1995 made up more than 24 per cent of gross domestic product, it employed about 37 per cent of labour force; more than fifty per cent of the population resides in rural areas and their material status is directly bound with the state of this leading sphere of the country's economic activity.

Perspectives of development, economic and financial condition of a number of branches of industry, including cotton-ginning, textile, light, food, chemical, farm machinery — about half of the overall industrial potential — during complex transition period directly depend on the agriculture. It is namely thanks to stable development of rural economy that industrial potential was sustained in recent years and even increased scale of production in branches associated with processing of farm produce. That is to say, the agrarian sector has grown into a powerful factor of economic stability in Uzbekistan.

Farm output, particularly cotton, is the principal currency earner and the main source feeding purchases of essential food products, medicine, oil and oil products, technology and technological equipment.

Hence, **problems of radical reformation and accelerated advancement of agrarian sector played a decisive role at the initial stage of reform and in the entire strategy of Uzbekistan's transition to market.**

We put forward the task to ensure priority development of the country-side and revive rural economy on qualitatively new principles. The whole process of reforming the country-side stemmed from the task of reviving the genuine master of the greatest wealth we possess — the land, and instilling hope in a farmer and making his life more prosperous. We strictly adhered to the principle that state is bound to render all-round assistance to the country-side. Persistently following these principles the Republic provided necessary conditions for reforming agrarian relations, restructuring agricultural enterprises, further increase of farm produce and reduce dependency on the import of some types of food products.

Along with earlier passed laws, Government resolutions adopted in February 1994 on additional measures on the realization of economic reform in rural economy, on further improvement of reform in live-stock breeding and protection of interests of dekhkan (peasant) farms and privatized farms, played a decisive role in accelerating the renovation process in the agrarian sector of economy.

A new economic structure which better fits the requirements of market economy has taken shape in rural areas as the result of moves undertaken in the course of agrarian reform. The non-state sector has expanded considerably in the country-side; the structure of agricultural production has changed noticeably and serious alterations have been introduced into the system of administration and methods of management.

The problem of ownership of land remains a key issue and the basis of the entire agrarian policy. The principal wealth of our country is land. It feeds us, it slakes thirst and creates main conditions for all vital activities. Hence the future of the country and the people will largely depend on how land use is organized in Uzbekistan.

The leading priority at the initial stage of economic reform was a change in the approach to land as the principal wealth. Decrees on rural questions, the Law "On Land" have outlined how to build relations in rural economy and how to deal with land. It is constitutionally confirmed that land cannot be sold for private tenure, however it can be transferred on conditions of long-term leasehold tenure.

Development of market relations in the country-side and the revival of the sense of proprietorship is affected by granting land for life tenure with the right to inherit it. The main objective was to introduce motivation of labour and such mechanism of farming which would provide a farmer an opportunity to freely dispose of the results of his own labour. We have drawn a clear-cut conclusion that only then a farmer feels himself a genuine master of his land when he is able to see that the fruit of his labour and the fruit of his land belong to him, that he is a true owner of the crop he had raised.

A peculiar feature of our agriculture is that basically it develops on irrigated lands supported by a powerful irrigation system. More than three fourths of all ploughlands are irrigated lands. That is why all perspectives of agricultural development are directly associated with the development of irrigated farming, construction and reconstruction of operating irrigation and land-reclamation systems, with the solutions of the question of who is going to own these systems. The most intense attention should be attached to problems of land improvement. Once we fail to accomplish this bow and our perspective is doomed.

There are 42 thousand hectares (ha) of irrigated lands and slightly more than 50 per cent of them are in proper meliorative condition, while the remaining areas require land-reclamation measures for their improvement. For this purpose 25 thousand ha of new lands are expected to be turned over for cultivation, 50 thousand ha will have to be reconstructed and collector-drainage network to be laid down on the area of 26.0 thousand ha.

Development of 1 ha of newly irrigated lands consumed 6.5 thousand roubles and reconstruction of traditionally irrigated lands — 5.0 thousand roubles back in 1990; these inputs make up currently 14-15 times that amount. It is obvious that not a single farmer is able to independently carry out irrigation and land reclamation operations. Only the state is capable to design and build land-reclamation networks and prevent soil from swamping, bogging and mineralization. A corresponding conclusion was drawn from the aforesaid, and today the state has taken responsibility for the implementation of all programmes related to land-reclamation, irrigation and raising soil fertility level thus rendering tremendous assistance and help to non-state farms.

Thorough analysis of development of economic relations and management organization system in the village disclosed the necessity of their radical reconsideration. Activities of collective and state farms were given critical re-evaluation at the initial stage of reform.

Our conclusion was that all state agricultural enterprises — state farms and, primarily, unprofitable ones would have to be reorganized into collective and other forms of ownership. This was predetermined by the need to put the country-side on firm economic rails. Actually that meant to straighten out those mistakes which had been committed in rural economy during preceding years in the sphere of agricultural management, when stemming dependency sentiments the collective farms were transformed into state farms in the hope for state support.

In the process of reorganization of management structures in the village, it became quite clear what primary farming chain had to look like. **It is a cooperative, uniting and rendering services to peasant farms, i.e. coordinating and securing logistic and technical assistance and rendering technical and agrotechnical services.**

Peasant farm should essentially serve as the basis for the organization of agricultural production, while to ensure its efficient operation there is to be a broad network of service infrastructure — agricultural firms, machine and tractor depots, repair shops, procurement stations, small business enterprises specializing in processing farm produce, etc.

Stemming from the principles and approaches elaborated at the first stage of economic reform, state farms were reorganized into collective, cooperative, share-holders and such other private agricultural enterprises. Since 1992 out of 1137 existing state farms 1066 have been transformed into joint-stock, collective and leasehold tenure enterprises. They served as the basis for establishment of 530 collective farms, about 350 cooperatives, more than 100 leasehold enterprises as well as enterprises with other forms of ownership. Apart from that 1516 live-stock farms have been turned over to their personnel's proprietorship. Currently the live-stock farms of agricultural enterprises not specialized in the output of live-stock produce are due for privatization and sale to private owners.

As a result the structure of agricultural production has considerably changed by the forms of proprietorship. The non-state sector has consolidated its position in the village. If in 1991 the share of state sector comprised 37 per cent of overall volume of agricultural production and that of non-state sector — 63 per cent, then in 1994 the non-state sector already produced 95 per cent of gross output.

The most significant result of the initial stage of economic reform in Uzbekistan was allotment of land under kitchen gardens, assignment of new, mostly irrigated lands under farmsteads and fruit-and-vegetable gardens through expansion of personal holdings of the population.

Allotment of people with land played a decisive role in the solution of the most urgent and acute problems during the first, the most crucial years of reform. On account of adopting cardinal measures on consolidating private land holdings we managed to:

first, attract excess, unemployed section of the population, primarily women and youth residing mostly in rural areas, to social productive labour, and thus relieve tension in the field of growing threat of mass unemployment;

second, increase real income of the population and strengthen social guarantees for many rural residents through issuing service record books to those engaged in production of farm output by agreements and granting them the right to old-age pension;

third, remove the acute problem of supply of the population with essential food products. Families allotted with land met their own needs in potato, vegetables, fruit and live-stock products. In addition, they expanded sales of their produce at urban markets and thus contributed their share to the solution of the problem of food supplies;

fourth, considerably expand the scale of individual housing construction, which promoted the solution of an acute problem of providing the population with housing and improvement of utility, communal and living conditions of the people;

and finally, fifth, secure socio-political stability in the Republic. This was not only on account of the removal of causes and sources of social conflicts but also as a result of active involvement of the population in the improvement of their individual holdings and fruit-and-vegetable gardens, engagement in social productive labour in the interests of their households and themselves, which distracted people from extremist political meetings.

Allotment of land to the people played a revolutionary role indeed, i.e. it eliminated each individual's dependency on the state. With land in his possession every man could make some profit, sense himself a proprietor and could feel himself free and independent.

More than 550 thousand ha of irrigated lands have been additionally allotted for the use of the people in the course economic transformations. This is considerably more than people possessed prior to adopting these resolutions. Total area of lands under personal holdings reached about 700 thousand ha. More than 9.0 million people enjoy the fruit of their land. The average area of personal holdings exceeds 0.2 ha, which in conditions of limited land resources is a tremendous achievement.

70 per cent of the overall number of live-stock, fifty per cent of sheep and goats is concentrated at personal holdings. The share of these holdings in the overall volume of agricultural production has increased from 30 to 44 per cent during the last three years. They produce (data of 1994) — 76 per cent of milk, 70 per cent of meat, 56 per cent of potato, 63 per cent of vegetables and 60 per cent of fruit in the country.

Great attention within the system of reform in rural economy at its first stage was attached to the development of new forms of organization of agricultural production meeting best the principles of acquiring the status of a genuine master of one's own land. A new dekhkan farm sector emerged and took shape in the village. Both legal and organizational prerequisites for stimulating the development of dekhkan farms were met. Farmers are entitled to long-term leaseland tenure of assigned land with the right to inherit it. Significant resources have been assigned from the national budget to render support to farmers.

Although, for Uzbekistan, cotton means political and economic power of the country, which guarantees the Republic's independence, we persistently conducted a policy on the elimination of hazardous impact of the cotton monopoly on the ecology and health of the people and on transfer of unproductive lands under cotton and other farm crops under the development of dekhkan farms.

Simultaneously was set up a system of protecting these farms through introducing government guarantees in their support and to raise fertility of lands. A system of rendering specialized services associated with machinery, fertilizers, seeds and saplings is being actively formed in the country-side to meet the needs of farmers. Veterinary and selection services have been restructured on the new principles. New trade points on the sale of seeds and planting material to farmers are opened in rural districts.

As a result, the number of dekhkan farms in 1994 increased 1.9 times over during one year alone and made up 25 thousand at the end of the year; among them more than 10 thousand farms specialize in the production of live-stock produce.

Total area of land under crops cultivated by dekhkan farms increased 2.7 times over in 1994 compared with 1993. Production of potato grew up 3 times over, that of potato, vegetables and melon crops — 3.3 times over, milk — 2.1 times and eggs — 1.3 times over. And this is the real result of the initial stage of expansion of dekhkan farms.

Intense attention at the initial stage of economic reform was devoted to the improvement of the structure of agricultural production. The vicious practices of administration imposing on farmers what to plant and where has been completely done away with. The farms are granted the right to independently determine the structure of land under cultivation and volume of production.

This was accompanied by raising procurement prices, persistent implementation of the policy on stabilization of cotton production, raising its yield and output of cotton fibre, on re-structuring released areas for cultivation of grain crops and potato through application of economic methods and motivation of labour.

The Republic was consistent in conducting a policy directed toward achieving grain independence and renewal of production of sugar and other food products. This course was successfully realized at the first stage, which is an exceptionally important result.

There has been a considerable change in the structure of land under cultivation in favour of significant expansion of lands under grain crops and respective reduction of plantations under cotton in connection with economic reform implemented in the Republic.

2.7 million tonnes of grain was produced in 1994, that is 44 per cent more than in 1991. In 1995 it is planned to produce more than 4.4 million tonnes of grain, including more than 3.5 million tonnes of wheat crops at all categories of farms. To ensure this, the area of lands under grain crops is to be increased up to 1 million 472 thousand ha, including up to 972 thousand ha of irrigated lands on account of further improvement of lands under crops and use of land released from cotton and feed crops.

Today we have been able not only to increase production of grain, but have managed to sharply reduce its import and re-distribute saved currency resources for solving other urgent tasks facing the Republic.

Plantations under potato are expected to be expanded up to 57 thousand ha bringing its production up to 800 thousand tonnes for which purpose it is planned to use high-quality Dutch seeds and utilize Dutch technology.

Apart from reforming relations of proprietorship in the village considerable attention at the initial stage was attached to perfection of mechanism of economic management. All this work focussed on three main directions.

First, introduction of just procurement prices on farm produce supplied for nation-wide needs became an important lever of stimulating the development of rural economy. With change in production conditions, procurement prices on practically all types of farm and live-stock produce were constantly raised for the purpose of raising the material well-being of farm workers.

Prices on cotton and grain have been considerably increased in recent years. Thus, if initially one tonne of cotton fibre cost 22 thousand roubles, then in 1994 the price of cotton equalled 3750 soums, or 170.5 times higher, while the harvest of 1995 is expected to be sold at the level of up to 50 per cent of world prices.

Procurement prices on potato, fruit and vegetables, live-stock and poultry, karakul (astrakhan) pelts and wool were also raised and **currently these and other types of output are sold at free (contract) prices.**

Raising procurement prices with their subsequent release of prices up to the level of free prices the state rendered practical assistance to rural economy and strived to secure price parity on industrial and farm produce.

Second, along with raising procurement prices the state continuously reconsidered its policy in the field of establishing government order on mandatory sale of farm produce for the needs of the state. Tangible results have been achieved in this sphere, too. In the first place government order on the majority of farm produce has been gradually cancelled. Today farms themselves are free to dispose of their output of live-stock breeding, vegetable growing, horticulture and viticulture.

Government order has been retained on cotton and grain, although in 1995 its amount is decreased down to 60 per cent for cotton and 50 per cent for grain. The objective is to abolish it too within the coming 2—3 years.

Increase of the volume of output retained by commodity producers for its free sale at their own option not only promoted economic consolidation of farms and improving the living standard of rural workers but also served as a powerful stimulus for expansion of output and development of businesses for their processing. Many farms have already established small business enterprises and shops for the manufacture and production of canned fruit, wines, flour, vegetable oil, cotton ginneries, etc.

Third, the state had elaborated and implemented measures on selective support of agricultural enterprises. Today all farms of the Republic are granted tax holidays on their profits, on value added tax and exempt from other taxes for two years after the establishment of dekhkan farms.

For the purpose of normalizing activities of farms credit accounts, debts and liabilities were more than once written off or clearing off earlier issued loans was delayed for three years.

Thus, at the first stage, inter-relations between farms and the state underwent significant changes which stimulated farmers interest in the result of their labour.

The most vital direction of agrarian policy conducted at the first stage and requiring its radical solution at subsequent stages of economic reform is a release of excess labour force currently employed in rural economy and drawing them into other sectors of economy — industry and the sphere of service.

Estimates show that 6.5 million people able to work are engaged in the village, which can hardly employ that much number of labour force. This explains an extremely slow rate of introduction of highly efficient industrial methods of agricultural production, advanced agrochemical methods and the result remains low efficiency and productivity of labour.

Hence the task of creating job opportunities on account of opening new mobile small businesses supplied with high technological equipment in rural areas retains its priority. These should not be merely enterprises on processing agricultural raw materials, but should include labour consuming enterprises with the use of home-workers and traditional crafts.

We have arrived at the conclusion that farms need small but high technological enterprises on primary processing of raw materials, which have to be built in areas with excess labour force.

Accelerated development of production and social infrastructure plays an important role within the system of measures on renovation and re-

arrangement of the village. This is one of the most crucial priorities of current agrarian policy. Only the establishment of a wide network of communal and engineering systems and radical improvement of social medium of rural residents can practically raise the agriculture to a qualitatively new level and attach it an industrial character.

At the same time this helps solve one of the key issues facing the village: to distract excess labour resources from the sphere of agricultural production proper to the sphere of industry and the sphere of rendering services to considerable number of able-bodied population.

Since the first day of its independence, Uzbekistan has been consistently implementing the purposeful programme of ensuring rural residents with fresh water and natural gas supplies. Thousands of kilometers of water mains and gas pipelines have been laid out within a short period of time and fresh water and gas were delivered to remote settlements and villages of Uzbekistan.

Nevertheless, the problems of establishing the modern network of production and social infrastructure and public utilities services have not been solved to the end.

Besides, the task of opening a broad network of small wholesale shops, repair shops and stations for supplying farmers with agricultural machinery, saplings, mineral fertilizers, etc. still remains an essential problem awaiting its solution.

It has to be admitted that agrarian reform is being implemented at insufficient rate and encounters numerous socio-economic problems and obstacles. They are linked, in the first place, with the process of breaking the mentality of dependents in agricultural production and placing it onto market foundation. There are still some administrators, managers and directors, expected to initiate reforms and actively conduct them, who have not yet succeeded in fully comprehending their new functions in the conditions of a market economy. There is still not enough understanding of new principles of economic management in the provinces; there is still lack of initiative and entrepreneurship at all levels of administration and management.

Despite organizational changes and economic benefits and incentives intra-economic production relations have not yet changed to a desirable extent. There are cases of ignoring the adopted laws and decrees and cases of infringement on the rights of manufacturers and producers. Little has been done to adjust the mechanism of inter-relationship of associated branches of economy — which is called upon to ensure efficient operation of rural economy.

Hence the principal task of a new stage in deepening agrarian reform should include the soonest possible eradication of the roots and causes hindering the course of reform; hampering complete modernization of agrarian relations in the village, first and foremost, relations of proprietorship, the establishment of agricultural firms and companies and the network of market and socio-production infrastructure; and placing obstacles on the way of raising technical level of agricultural production. Farmers need reliable legal guarantees protecting their interests

The most important in the chain of these tasks is to exert every effort to bring up and firmly establish in the minds of producers of farm output the sense of a master-proprietor.

1.5. INSTITUTIONAL TRANSFORMATIONS AND ELIMINATION OF ADMINISTRATIVE-COMMAND SYSTEM OF MANAGEMENT

Transition to market economy, renovation of economic relations requires the implementation of institutional transformations and the establishment of a corresponding system of administration and management. That explains why so much attention at the first stage of economic reform was attached to reforming the system of administration and management.

There is now every ground to state that the reform of administration and management has been implemented in general and successfully enough. The results of this reform will have to be yet seriously analyzed and corresponding conclusions must be drawn. But some of these conclusions are obvious even now.

In the course of the first stage, there was implemented a complicated and at times painful transition from totalitarian to democratic system, from centrally distributive to market mechanism of distribution, from tough policy of directive command administration to self-administration and self-regulation on the basis of economic motivation and stimulation. Practically at that stage was created a new system of administration and management.

We never had any corresponding or similar experience in the past. Study and research into the system of administration and management in the countries with established or establishing market relations prompted us to work out our own system using the most acceptable structures of national macro- and micro-economic management which fit best present conditions prevailing in Uzbekistan.

Our approaches were mostly of an experimental nature. But these experiments were quite bold, since it seemed to be the only way to resolutely get rid of the chains of a discredited administrative-command system and to introduce as fast as possible a new institutional system meeting rapidly changing economic conditions.

Already in the course of institutional transformations, we improved mechanisms of management, elaborated such organizational and legal forms of managing the sectors and spheres of economy to the greatest extent corresponded their specifics, promoted the introduction of economic liberties for economic entities and stimulated the development of initiative and entrepreneurship. Rejection of centralized planning and production organization and of state regulation of financial and material flows required the search of principally new approaches to the organization of economic management.

A consistent and gradual model of organization of management was adopted for the system of further improvement of production management. The process of management system reform passed several stages and is still in progress.

As a result of structural changes in the sphere of management, numerous administrative and managerial structures changed their functions and were replaced by new organs. Remaining elements of command-administrative control and auditing systems and their executive agencies were completely abolished. Their distributive functions and mechanisms were cancelled.

The activity of central economic organs and ministries is being radically re-organized. The functions and tasks which they are authorized to solve are being drastically changed.

Symbols of the unshakable and eternal nature of the centralized planning system, the core of an administrative-command and bureaucratic system — State Planning Commission, State Committee on Logistics and Supplies, State Committee on Prices, State Committee of Agro-Industry — these and such other state committees and ministries with huge bureaucratic personnel have been abolished.

New structures have been established to counterweigh them and initiate and introduce new market relations. Thus, for notorious State Planning Commission was replaced by the State Committee on Forecasting and Statistics. With consideration of principles and priorities of economic reform and mechanism of its realization, this Committee is authorized to: evaluate the course of economic reform and advance proposals on its further deepening; carry out analytical analysis on the basis of macro-economic balance account and changes of tendencies in sectoral and territorial structures; provide multi-optional forecast of socio-economic development of the country, branches and sectors of economy, as well as provinces stemming from the need of ensuring Uzbekistan's economic independence.

In place of the State Committee on Logistics and Supplies, a monopolistic distributive monster, and its successor "Uzcontracttrade", was established a new market structure — Republican Joint-Stock Association of Wholesale and Stock Exchange Trade for the purpose of creating proper infrastructure for free and equitable participation of commodity manufacturers, consumers and entrepreneurs at the commodity market. Structurally it incorporates the Republican Joint-Stock Commodity Exchange, Share-Holders Exchange Bank and territorial Share-Holders Commercial-Mediator companies. They are authorized to render enterprises, organizations and legal persons irrespective of their form of proprietorship commercial, mediatory, trade, marketing and such other services on a contract and mutually-agreed basis and create equitable conditions for participation in stock exchange deals.

In conditions of price liberalization, the State Committee on Prices was completely abolished and a special Main Directorate on Demonopolization and Control of High Monopolistic Prices was instituted within the structure of the Ministry of Finance. Its principal objective is to counter the formation of monopolistic structures and promote creation of competitive environment in the country.

The role of financial and banking structures changes radically in conditions of transition to market economy. Center of gravity on state regulation of market relations shifted mainly on these key structures. That is to say, they are called upon to elaborate and conduct a co-ordinated fiscal and monetary policy on which will depend the state of economy in general.

This predetermined significant changes in the function and structure of the Ministry of Finance and Central Bank of the Republic of Uzbekistan in recent years. Along with the formation of the national budget the Ministry of Finance is authorized to elaborate basic guidelines and principles of tax policy of the state and conduct a co-ordinated financial policy and currency regulation.

the Office of the President with its corresponding control inspectorates within the structure of provincial governor's administrations.

As it was mentioned earlier, the Inter-Departmental Council on Economic Reform, Entrepreneurship and Foreign Investments under the President was established for co-ordination of activities for accelerated implementation of economic reform.

At the first stage, one of the leading objectives was practical formation of a multi-structural economy and revival of private, non-state sector of economy. For the purpose of meeting this objective, the Government established State Committee on Management of State Property and Support of Entrepreneurship, which was empowered to conduct a coordinated policy in the formation of multi-structural economy and render support to entrepreneurship, identify priorities in the decentralization process and advance draft programmes of privatization and development of private businesses.

A special fund of the State Committee was designed to mobilize financial resources, in-coming from transformation of state property into other forms of proprietorship, with their subsequent channelling to the solution of tasks of structural re-organizations in economy and to support enterprises during the post-privatization period. The State Committee on Property promotes and takes direct part in the establishment of investment funds, consulting and auditing agencies, holding societies, stock exchanges and real estate markets and such other market structures.

The most important guideline of institutional transformations at the first stage was the establishment of administrative structures authorized to ensure the development and consolidation of external relations. In this connection for the first time in the history of the country was instituted Ministry of External Economic Relations authorized to carry out regular analyses of international markets of goods and services, to elaborate strategy in the sphere of external economic activity, to maintain centralized export-import deliveries of produce and coordinate activities of all external economic organizations and agencies of the Republic.

The deepest structural changes took place in the system of management of sectors and individual spheres of the Republic's economy.

With the disintegration of the Soviet Union, abolishment of All-Union ministries and nationalization of enterprises with the all-union and union-republican status located in the territory of Uzbekistan, the problem of organization of their administration and management acquired special significance. They have been voluntarily united into state sectoral concerns depending on their profiles. This not only enables the preservation of production potential, but it gives a new impetus to their development.

Later, when enterprises were provided with greater economic freedom, state concerns were transformed into branch associations while financing of their administrative staff was effected on account of voluntary deductions of their affiliates.

In the course of the first stage of reform, all branch ministries were fully dismantled through their re-organization into associations, concerns, corporations, unions and other economic amalgamations. Restructuring affected automobile transport, civil engineering and rural economy.

Concerns, associations and corporations are voluntary amalgamations of enterprises and organizations on the basis of community of their economic interests irrespective of their department subordination and forms of proprietorship. They organize their activities on account of their entrance fees and packages of shares.

National companies were established in branches and spheres of nation-wide significance, namely tourism, transport, culture, film distribution, etc. Their complete economic independence is a specific feature of these companies. They work in conditions of self-financing and independently solve questions of production, economic, and financial activity.

The basic tasks of associations, concerns, corporations and other amalgamations during transition period was and remains to supply national economy of the country with concrete types of manufactured output, to carry out a unified scientific-technical and investment policy, to analyse the state of external and domestic markets, to develop market relations in their respective sectors, to organize activities on transformation of state enterprises and organizations into non-state forms of proprietorship and to render all-round support to development of entrepreneurship. Besides, these economic amalgamations ensure legal protection of their founders interests and represent them at the state and local organs of administration and determine a strategy of their respective sectors development.

Work had started in 1994 on their re-organization into holding companies and other organizations of corporate management. Apart from that their affiliates themselves decide what form and method of amalgamation to choose.

We took to the new style of activity after organizations and enterprises at grass-root level had been provided with greater economic freedom and the state cancelled the imposition of its dictat on them. Enterprises were granted the right to independently organize production and sale of their produce. Moreover, the realization of the principle of providing equal conditions for enterprises with differing forms of ownership was ensured not only de jure but de facto as well.

A peculiar feature of shaping market relations is a shift of the center of all activities' gravity directly to provinces in the formation of multi-structural economy, privatization of state property, accelerated development of productive forces and in solving the problem of raising the well-being of the people. Territorial aspects of market transformations gain momentum. Under these conditions the role and responsibility of local administrations in the solution of tasks facing them has been raised and their structure changed.

In compliance with the Law "On Re-organization of Local Bodies of Administration in the Republic of Uzbekistan" in January 1992 was introduced the institute of khokims (governors) who had representative and executive administrations at provincial, district and municipal levels. They are called upon to solve all problems of local significance stemming from state-wide interests and the interests of local residents.

Local administrations form executive offices under khokims to solve current tasks which in the past were effected by local councils of people's deputies and executive committees.

The experience of institutional transformations and reforming the system of management at the initial stage of transition to market relations prompted the following conclusions.

First, it was extremely vital at the initial stage not to destroy seriously the system of administration, not to lose managerial control of economics, something which happened in a number of CIS states, since newly-organized organs had neither experience nor the very mechanism of self-regulation in market conditions.

Second, in the course of transition period, when market relations and mechanism had not matured to the end, economic methods alone could not operate efficiently without application of certain administrative levers. There is no doubt that priority goes with legal norms and economic methods, however, sometimes there is a need in reasonable administrative regulation, particularly so in the interests of maintaining executive and financial order.

Third, re-organization of administrative organs and granting them new functions did not mean that reformation of administration and management was completed. It is the style of work that is required to be radically changed and those administrative and management structures to the full extent met modern conditions and principles of organization of economic advancement and production.

Fourth, destruction of vertical and horizontal organizational and economic links predetermined not merely by the collapse of the former Soviet Union but mostly by accelerated rates of economic reform, decentralization and privatization could not by itself change the departmental and bureaucratic nature of administrative and management structures.

Hence, one of the principal tasks today is a resolute struggle against formalism, impertinent bureaucratism, inertia, and stagnation still surviving in a number of administrative and management organs.

Fifth, formation of new administrative and management structures makes higher demands on the qualification of their staff. Modern administrative personnel and managers will have to be not only highly professional but have a broad erudite mind, be a competent and initiative person with a sense of responsibility for his job, be capable to solve problems in creative way, but most importantly be a true patriot of his Fatherland.

1.6. LIBERALIZATION OF PRICES AND SHAPING OF MARKET INFRASTRUCTURE

Particular significance during transition from centralized planning system and administrative-command distributive system to market mechanisms of economic progress is attached to the problem of price release and its adjustment with production costs and actual demand on raw and output.

Free market prices formed on the basis of actual demand and supply are a major link of market economy, which ensures close interaction and cooperation between output manufacturers and consumers. In the introduction of civilized market conditions the mechanism of free price-formation provides an opportunity to combine optimally the interests of individual commodity manufacturers, consumers and the society on the whole in the course of production, exchange, distrubution and consumption of goods.

Price liberalization is a key issue of economic reform upon the solution of which largely depends on the question of along which direction the process of reform will develop and what socio-economic consequences it will lead to. Namely this difference in approaches to price liberalization, bringing domestic prices into line with world prices, ensuring price balance between separate types of raw and output, between prices and level of population's and enterprises' income largely predetermine the difference between known models of transition from planned to market economy. And the range of these approaches is broad enough — from extraordinary, "shocking" price release up to artificial freezing of prices and preservation of state regulation and price control.

Various options have been considered in Uzbekistan in the process of selecting ways for the realization of this task. Moreover, paramount significance in out conditions is attached, primarily to consideration of possible negative consequences of price release.

Both extremes were unacceptable for us. They met neither real conditions nor the material position of the greater strata of the population nor the objectives of our course of reform. We got thoroughly prepared for the change of the entire price system, adopted a critical approach fully realizing our responsibility for the destiny of the nation and economy of the country.

Perhaps the choice of approaches, tactics and strategy of price liberalization concretely revealed, as never before, one of the principles of economic reform — gradualness and the stage-by-

stage nature of reforms carried out in the Republic.

By 1990 the price system was completely disbalanced and could not ensure equal and just exchange between different regions and republics of the ex-Soviet Union. Prices of the output of raw-producing sectors and rural economy, as a rule, were artificially reduced, while that on the output of processing industries — artificially increased. Under the then external trade balance with the countries of the former Soviet Union, when the republic exported, as a rule, at low prices raw and farm products and imported finished goods and consumer commodities, Uzbekistan incurred colossal losses and was artificially placed in the position of a subsidized republic. This not only inflicted economic damage but also was quite immoral in respect to our rich country and its people.

Because of distortions in price formation, whole sectors of economy and regions of the country found themselves in extremely difficult situation. Particularly difficult was the situation in rural economy. Back from the times of mass industrialization in the ex-USSR were retained the so-called "price scissors" on industrial and farm produce. As a result of reduced prices which did not match real inputs of labour and demand on agricultural produce many farms were planned to be unprofitable, failed to cover their current costs and could neither compensate for the hard labour of farmers nor ensure supplies of machinery, seeds, material resources and financial means for the development of social sphere. About 65 per cent of population in Uzbekistan are rural residents who were compelled to live in poverty and destitution.

More than that, efficient material stimuli and motivation of labour, care of land, machinery and the very farm produce — cotton, grain, etc — were discredited and undermined.

Prices were artificially reduced on commodity goods, separate types of raw materials, particularly oil, electricity and other power utilities; transport and public utility rates resulted in their excessive consumption, while actual cost failed to be covered by their profits. In the past the difference between prices, rates and production cost of output and services were covered on account of budget allocations or "cross-subsidies" of one category of consumers by another.

Under these conditions a considerable part of economic entities incurred big losses, which required an increase of state inputs to maintain their activity. In this connection producers were reimbursed part of their expenses on production of grain, flour and other food products from national budget, and losses from granting various social benefits also were compensated on account of government resources. Moreover, resources for the manufacture of a number of goods for children, medicine and a wide range of public services were donated from state budget. In 1991 alone about 4 billion roubles or more than 12 per cent of national budget was spent to compensate for difference in prices and to subsidize unprofitable enterprises.

Apart from that, significant difference in prices on the similar types of produce at domestic and world markets seriously hindered the establishment of mutually-beneficial external economic relations and formation of a progressive structure of foreign trade. On the other hand, the aspiration to integrate with the world economic system as soon as possible put newly independent states in a position to liberalize prices on many types of raw and materials and transport service rates. This in turn served as a powerful and inevitable factor of growing inflation processes in these countries.

All this was required to select weighted, accurately calculated approaches to the implementation of price reform, transformation of the entire system of price-formation and prevention of a disastrous spiral of hyperinflation.

A number of newly independent states, which emerged from countries of the former socialist camp, selected the road of "shock therapy" and at once released prices on all types of raw materials, consumer commodities and services, the result was that in Poland consumer prices increased 9 times over, in Yugoslavia — 13 times and in Russia — 26 times over.

A sharp and extraordinary rise in prices on raw materials under practically uncompetitive levels of technology and equipment, even with liberalization of prices on finished products, placed enterprises in a critical position and turned them into low profitable and unprofitable endeavors.

This again resulted in sharp impoverishment of the population and deterioration of social situation. Active liberalization of prices and lack of competition from quite a number of enterprises and farms led to rapid decline in production, as imported products squeezed them out of domestic markets, and national industry and rural economy collapsed.

Taking into account the high level of interrelation between the economy of Uzbekistan and Russia and other republics of the former Soviet Union sharing the same currency, we were compelled to start price liberalization within the rouble zone. But our approach was based on our own principles of reform with consideration of the real situation and existing living standard of the population.

We categorically rejected "shocking" methods and despite strong outside pressure we made the decision to carry out the process of price liberalization gradually, in compliance with the planned scenario. Such an approach allowed enterprises and the population to adapt without "shocks" to conditions of market relations and free price-formation.

Considerable changes took place in Uzbekistan from 1991 to 1994 in the field of price liberalization. Fixed prices were transformed into free prices practically on all types of raw materials and finished products; a direct government price control on all consumer commodities were fully abolished during that period.

At the same time, starting from January of 1992 price liberalization was carried out in stages. Small steps wre taken allowing strong preventive moves for social protection of the population.

Transition to contract (free) prices and rates on a wide range of production-technical items, separate types of consumer commodities, operations and services was carried out in Uzbekistan beginning January 10, 1992 in accordance with the government Resolution "On Measures on Liberalization of Prices".

The Government of the Republic established price limits on a limited list of food and industrial goods and introduced rate limits on certain types of services rendered to the population with the objective to protect the interests of the population. In this connection producers of grain, bread, flour and other food products were reimbursed from the national budget. The state also covered expenses for providing free breakfasts and allowances to school-children and students. Certain types of goods for children and medicine were also subsidized from the budget.

The range and list of commodities and services realized at fixed and regulated prices was substantially reduced in 1993. The specific feature of price liberalization in 1993 was that state regulation of contract wholesale prices was abolished. Norms and rates of maximum profitability level which covered only basic types of fuel-and-power complex products still in force in 1992 were also eliminated.

The period between October and November of 1994 marked a significant stage in the process of price liberalization. Prices on major types of consumer commodities were released and rates for transport and public utility services were raised. Prices on bread and flour were still subsidized, as well as housing and public utility services and public urban transport. Thus, the first stage of economic reform was completed, with full liberalization of prices causing no social shocks. The state secured reliable protection of the interests of the population through establishment of various compensation funds, introduction of child-care allowances, regular increase of minimum salaries, pensions and stipends, rendering material assistance to those in need through makhallya (neighbourhood) committees and introduction of a number of tax benefits, when 50 per cent of compensation costs were covered on account of reducing the level of deductions into the budget and through other forms of reimbursements.

If we look at transition to market merely from the point of prevalence of free prices in economy, then the conclusion will be that Uzbekistan already lives in conditions of market relations.

A purposeful policy on the formation of a competitive environment in the economy was implemented throughout the entire period of stage-by-stage price liberalization in the country. With this aim in view a Law of the Republic of Uzbekistan "On Restriction of Monopolistic Activity" was adopted in August 1992 and a package of normative documents directed towards the development of competitive environment was elaborated and implemented on its basis.

The Main Directorate on Anti-Monopoly and Price Policy was established within the structure of the Ministry of Finance for carrying out active anti-monopoly measures and its was granted the right to regulate prices and profitability of monopoly enterprises by having output registered in the national and provincial register-books. Currently the list of monopolists includes 658 enterprises manufacturing 1625 different commodities. At the same time, problems of anti-monopoly regulation and formation of a genuinely competitive environment constitute basic tasks of a new stage of economic reform.

Shaping of market relations is unthinkable without corresponding environment — market infrastructure, which is called upon to promote inter-

relation between economic entities at the commodity, currency and labour markets.

The centralized system of administration and management of the past, despite all its disadvantages and shortcomings was integral and complete in its own way. Destruction of existing established organizational and economic ties, predetermined not as much by the disintegration of the former Soviet Union but rather by accelerated processes of decentralization and privatization in Uzbekistan could not by itself change the departmental and bureaucratic nature of distribution of output, material and financial resources which took shape during several decades.

A factor of principle was how, when, by what means, and in what form transition from centralized planning system of distribution of all types of resources (financial, raw, commodity and labour — to market system) would be carried out. In other words, the task we faced then was the introduction of parallel markets of commodities and services, raw materials, capital and labour.

The first step toward market starts with the establishment of a market infrastructure: solution of problems of financial, banking and credit systems; institution of insurance, auditing, legal and consulting firms and companies and a system of exchanges.

It is impossible to set up an infrastructure all at once. It is a continuous and complicated process which requires highly professional personnel and psychological adaptation of economic entities and the population to new conditions of economic activity.

The first step toward shaping a market infrastructure was the elimination of the system of

mandatory state order on the delivery of output and centralized supplies of funds and resources for its manufacture. In the course of the first stage of reform, state order was gradually replaced by purchases at contract (free) prices of output required for meeting the needs of the state, such as those associated with ensuring security of the country, socially significant requirements and export of produce in compliance with inter-governmental commitments.

The elimination of state order brought about the abolishment of former structures in charge of centralized distribution of commodity resources. Their place was filled with structures called upon to promote the establishment of commodity market. The Republican commodity exchange in 1994 alone concluded more than one thousand contracts amounting to more than 1.3 billion soums.

A system of commodity and raw exchange developed dynamically in the Republic. At the time of its introduction in mid-1991, the first sales were held at the first commodity-stock exchange "Toshkent". By the next year there were more than three dozen operating exchanges incorporated into the Union of Exchanges.

The establishment of an exchange system of commodity resource distribution entailed the emergence of numerous entrepreneurship structures — brokers and dealers offices, trade houses, intermediator firms. A niche in the economy occupied fully by state distributive organs in the past, gradually let in representatives of the newly-emerging market structure. This marked a decisive step toward replacement of former distributive structures with a new mechanism.

With the realization of the "privatization minor" programme, practically the whole network of trade and public services establishments were decentralized and intermediator firms and offices sprang up with new channels of commodity flows.

Another guideline of market infrastructure formation was the establishment of structures designed to ensure operation of capital market. A new system was created to effect financial and monetary-credit regulation.

The credit resource market activated its operations beginning in 1994. Interest rates had an increasing impact on re-distribution of financial resources among sectors of national economy and enterprises of the Republic. The introduction of credit resources and distribution of credits on a competitive basis was one of the corner-stones in the emergence of a financial market.

The procedure for participation of organizations involved in external economic activity and weekly currency sales at inter-bank currency exchange has been recently considerably simplified. The amount of currency for sale has noticeably increased. All real conditions are present for holding currency auctions twice a week and even more frequently.

Insurance companies have displayed even greater activity in the financial market. The former "Gosstrah" (State Insurance Committee) of the Republic and its functions were transformed and its place is currently filled with more than forty non-governmental insurance companies operating in the form of joint-stock companies. The process of insuring political and commercial risks, bank and exchange transactions has taken effected in the Republic.

World experience has it that in conditions of transition to market relations the problem of growing unemployment will become rather acute. The problem of unemployment is one of the key issues in the system of macro-economic regulation and within the entire economic policy of industrialized countries with well-established structure of market economy. Its acuity particularly increases in conditions of production decline or in the course of broad and mass privatization, which is a peculiar feature of the initial phase of transformation of economic systems, when not only unqualified people fall into the rank of unemployed but also specialists with popular and rare professions since, although temporarily, there is limited demand for their occupation.

Of paramount significance under these conditions is the issue of shaping a full-blooded labour market, registration of all those looking for a job and taking stock of available vacancies. Taking into consideration the current demographic situation when average annual population grows equals to more than 2 per cent, when there is an excess labour force in the country-side, small towns and settlements, and when "hidden" unemployment in some industries is a reality we attach great attention to the system of employment agencies and training of personnel. Inadmissibility of growing unemployment was one of principal tasks at the first stage of economic reform which was successfully solved.

A wide network of labour exchange (the system has one labour exchange in each district, 240 in all) was established in the Republic. A procedure of registration of unemployed persons, their professional re-orientation and effecting unemployment allowance payments was worked out. The result is that officially registered unemployed make up less than one per cent of labour resources. This is, indeed, an impressive result of the first stage of reform in conditions of our Republic.

Thus, the result of the first stage of economic reform was the shaping of basic outlines of required market infrastructure ensuring operation of emerging national and provincial markets of the Republic, as well as regulation of inter-state economic relations.

1.7. LIBERALIZATION OF EXTERNAL ECONOMIC ACTIVITY AND INTEGRATION WITH THE WORLD ECONOMIC COMMUNITY

The most important result of the first stage of economic reform is a break through in the decades-long isolation of Uzbekistan's economy, and the elaboration and implementation of independent foreign economic policy.

The years of independence were the years of creating necessary political, legal and organizational foundations for setting up the basis of an open economy. State monopoly of the former Soviet Union on foreign trade collapsed after the elimination of a totalitarian regime and, with it all legal norms regulating external relations, the All-Union system of centralized organization of export and import operations and the regulation of re-distribution of currency resources at the union level.

Disintegration of All-Union foreign trade and external economic structures, their absolute absence in the Republic, lack of knowledge on the situation in the world market and acute shortage of qualified specialists with experience in foreign trade caused a number of difficulties in conducting foreign policy. Volume of export and inflow of hard currency went down; Uzbek exporters were forced out from their traditional markets. Spontaneous and massive dumping of produce to the world market by the republics of the former Soviet Union in 1992 led to a sharp fall in world prices on cotton-fibre, gold, non-ferrous metals, oil and other raw materials.

The existing situaton prompted the formation at accelerated rates of our own system of foreign economic management, the elaboration of our own principles of establishing external ties and independently determined ways of integrating Uzbekistan into the world economic system. This advanced the task of gradual liberalization of foreign economic activity with rapid reduction of administrative restrictions and their substitution with international norms and rules and market tools of foreign trade regulation.

During the years of independence we have elaborated and consistently implemented the basic principles of our foreign policy. They primarily sterm from Uzbekistan's aspiration to build its foreign policy on the principles of equality and mutual benefit, non-interference into internal affairs of other states. We firmly hold to the principle not to enter into the sphere of influence of any state and henceforward are determined to independently define our inter-relations with all countries of the world irrespective of their ideological doctrines. We have been consistently following the principle of establishing both bilateral and multilateral mutually-beneficial relations through deepening cooperation within the framework of international economic unions, in which Uzbekistan accepted membership and is an active participant in their work.

As a sovereign state, Uzbekistan puts much effort to form an open economy. Broad involvement of a country in the world economic relations and international division of labour is the basis for building open-type economy. Carrying out consistent measures on deepening economic reform and shaping a socially-oriented market economy, we realize the indisputable fact that market economy is a free economy of an open nature and that isolationism and separatism are alien to it. In this contex the future of our economy is visualized in integration with the world economy.

It is not a coincidence that one of the decisive legal steps in ensuring genuine sovereignty of the Republic was constitutional consolidation of Uzbekistan as an independent entity of international relations determining its foreign policy in its own interests with the right to accept membership in international organizations, systems of collective security and inter-state formations.

All this, in its turn, was a consolidation of practical achievement. To date Uzbekistan has been recognized by more than 150 countries of the world: 74 of them established diplomatic relations with our Republic, Embassies of more than 30 countries have been opened and started work in the capital of Uzbekistan, among them embassies of leading world nations: United States, Japan, Germany, UK, France and China. Diplomatic missions of our country are accredited already in more than 20 countries of the world (United States, Germany, France, Turkey, India, Russia, etc.).

The Republic of Uzbekistan actively switched in to multi-lateral international mechanisms of economic cooperation, joined and is an active member of a number of prestigious international financial and economic institution. These include the United Nations and its agencies, the World Bank, International Monetary Fund, International Finance Corporation, Organization for Promotion of Economic Cooperation, International Labour Organization, World Health Organization and other leading financial-economic organizations.

A number of international organizations — UNO, UMF, World Bank, European Bank for Reconstruction and Development, Commission of European Community, etc. opened their regional offices and actively cooperate with their Uzbek partners.

A programme of system transformations has been elaborated jointly with the IMF experts designed to reform deeply the economy of Uzbekistan. The first transfer amounting to US$ 74 million was already effected for the realization of this programme. Work is underway today on assigning the same amount to Uzbekistan for the evaluation of possible elaboration and implementation of "Stand-by" programme in this country.

The question of providng Uzbekistan with a rehabilitation loan, amounting to US$ 160 million, was worked out jointly with the World Bank and an agreement was signed on channelling these resources for consolidation of national currency, expansion of external economic activity and backing up the balance of payments, carrying out structural transformations of economy and implementation of reform at enterprise level, and for rendering necessary assistance and back up to decentralized enterprises in the post-privatization period and to newly emerging non-governmental structures.

A number of projects elaborated with participation of the IMF, World Bank and the IFC are being implemented, which promote, in particular, the development of small and medium businesses in the Republic and financial support of projects in top-priority sectors of economy.

Uzbekistan and the states of Central Asia joined the Organization of Economic Cooperation established by Turkey, Iran and Pakistan. Within its framework, the Republic actively participates in the elaboration and realization of projects on joint construction of inter-state transport communications, ensuring Uzbekistan an access to sea ports, to transnational transport networks and world commodity and capital markets.

In June 1994 Uzbekistan was granted the status of an observer at the General Agreement on Tariffs and Trade (GATT) which holds central position in the regulation of modern system of world trade. Negotiations are going on now about Uzbekistan's acceptance of membership in GATT as a full member which will open up the Republic a prospect of trading with 111 countries — full members of this Agreement on the solid legal basis and enjoy certain privileges.

To maintain and implement the programme of economic reform, the international organizations and 21 donor-countries render Uzbekistan an extensive technical assistance, which in 1993—1994 was evaluated at the level of about US$ 75 million. This technical assistance was channelled for training specialists, improving the system of economic management and the system of state regulation of transition to market, for human resource development and the development of the power system and transport, for rendering technical and humanitarian assistance in the field of health services, for medical supplies and protection of the environment, for consolidation of financial, tax and banking systems and computerization of various spheres of economy.

Besides, resources assigned in the form of technical assistance are envisaged to be directed for elaboration of draft laws on private sector, privatization and decentralization of production, reorganization of accounting system, improvement of the system of social protection of the population and for the implementation of other tasks of paramount importance for this Republic and its people.

It has to be noted that Uzbekistan's cooperation with international organizations was built and will be built with consideration of an objective combining both long-term and current priorities.

First, this is an "integration" task — direct involvement in international monetary, financial and trade mechanisms on the basis of establishment of equitable conditions meeting national interests of the country for ensuring cooperation of all economic entities of Uzbekistan with the outside world.

Second, this means direct assistance in the solution of urgent issues, facing the Republic, support of reform process through receiving financial, technical and consultative assistance on the part of a number of aforesaid institutions on the basis of accumulated international experience.

At the initial stage of economic reform, we had to begin the establishment of modern foreign economic complex of the Republic practically from point zero and created actually a new mechanism of regulation of external economic activity. The reform of Uzbekistan's foreign economic relations advanced noticeably, in the first place, in its organizational and legal aspects.

Practically anew have been created all necessary republican institutional structures: Ministry of External Economic Relations, National Bank of External Economic Activity and the Customs Service. Corresponding foreign economic departments have been established and operate currently in the Cabinet of Ministers, ministries and agencies, corporations, concerns, associations, and provincial administrations. A Republican International Trade Centre is being established with the participation of foreign partners. We opened trade houses in a number of foreign countries. Bilateral trade and industrial chambers have been established between Uzbekistan and the United States, UK, Germany and other countries interested in active cooperation with our Republic.

The composition and structure of participants in foreign economic relations altered since the beginning of economic reform. More than two thousand economic entities of the Republic, including associations, concerns, small and private enterprises have been granted the right to direct access to external market.

Apart from external trade, other forms of foreign economic cooperation develop ever more dynamically; the number of established and operating enterprises with foreign investments continue to grow in the Republic. Currently the number of registered enterprises with foreign capital in the territory of the Republic exceeds 1450, among them 110 are enterprises with purely foreign capital. By 1995 there were 166 representations of foreign firms, banks and companies from 25 countries in Uzbekistan. The National Bank of External Economic Activity opened correspondence accounts with 80 major world banks.

Basic legal acts, Presidential Decrees and government Resolutions were adopted during the first years of independence which laid a legal foundation for expansion of external relations and liberalization of entire foreign economic activity and has stimulated the development of the Republic's export potential. These include the Laws "On External Economic Activity", "On Foreign Investments and Guarantees of Foreign Investors' Activity", and other legal and normative acts, which enabled the setting up of basic framework conditions for effecting external economic activities, for concluding and execution of international agreements in the sphere of foreign economic relations, ensure protection of the economic interests of the Republic, legal persons and citizens of Uzbekistan abroad, and to establish legal guarantees for the activity of foreign investors in the territory of the Republic.

A number of benefits were introduced for the purpose of stimulation the expansion of foreign economic relations. First and foremost, customs taxes for import of commodities were abolished and customs duties for export of the own output were considerably reduced. Moreover, export produce of joint ventures is exempt from customs tax. Instead of tax on currency proceeds mandatory sale of its part was introduced, amounting to 30 per cent, to the Central Bank of the Republic. Many enterprises were exempt from compulsory sale of part of the currency revenues with the aim of stimulating their interest in channelling currency receipts from export of the output to expansion of their material basis and their export potential.

Considerably simpler was made the procedure of establishment of joint ventures with the participation of foreign capital, registration of participants in foreign economic activity and licensing of exportable produce. In 1994 alone the list of items due to export licensing shrank from 74 to 11. All this had a positive impact on the activation of foreign economic activity and on the improvement of export-import structure.

Foreign trade was carried out in two directions at the first stage of reform with the CIS states on the basis of inter-governmental agreements and with foreign countries with settling accounts in freely convertible currency. The establishment of direct foreign economic cooperation was also highly encouraged.

Gross foreign trade turnover in 1994 increased against the previous year's level and made up US$ 5,053.3 million, including US$ 2,919.7— with the CIS states and US$ 2,133.6— with foreign countries. The share of trade with foreign countries increased significantly in the gross foreign trade turnover.

In 1992 export of produce to foreign countries equalled US$ 870 million, in 1993 US$ 920 million and in 1994 — more than US$ 1.000 million.

Currently a considerable portion of export falls, apart from traditional CIS partners, on Turkey, Belgium, UK, France, the Netherlands, Poland, Republic of Korea, Indonesia, Malaysia, etc.

We attach intense attention to consolidation and development of multilateral ties and close cooperation with the Central Asian states. Indeed, brotherly nations of Central Asia are bound by common history, cultural traditions, way of life, mentality and many other features. Problems of present-day life — political, economic, cultural and economic ones — are identical in all Central Asian countries. The economies of these republics are mutually-integrated and inter-connected.

Taking the existing realities into consideration an agreement on the establishment of a single economic area between the republics of Uzbekistan and Kazakhstan was signed during the meeting with President Nazarbaev on January 10, 1994 in Tashkent. Among others were also signed inter-governmental agreements on deepening cooperation in the field of science, education, culture, health services, tourism and sport. The agreements envisage free transfer of goods, commodities, capital and labour between Uzbekistan and Kazakhstan and coordinated conduct of credit, accounts, budgetary, tax, price, customs and monetary policies. Kyrghyzstan joined this agreement at the summit meeting in Bishkek, and this opened up still greater perspectives for deepening integration process in the Central Asian region.

The Agreement on a single economic area between three states has already started bearing its fruit. An Inter-State Executive Committee made up of representatives of participating countries was established in Almaty, a regional banking centre started in operations in Tashkent. A programme of industrial integration was worked out which serves the basis for the elaboration of concrete projects of joint investments into manufacture of produce needed most in the Central Asian countries.

One of the top-priority trends in our foreign policy is the development of direct friendly and multi-lateral relations with the countries making up the Commonwealth of Independent States. Uzbekistan supported the idea of the Commonwealth, joined the ranks of its founders and works actively on the consolidation of relations of integration and cooperation. Uzbekistan takes an active part in the formation of institutional structures of Economic Commonwealth — Inter-State Economic Committee, Inter-State Bank, etc. Bilateral foreign political, trade, economic and other treaties and agreements have been signed within the framework of the Commonwealth with Russia, Ukraine, Belarus, Moldova and other CIS countries which lay a solid foundation for close mutually-beneficial cooperation.

The structure and nature of economic relations changes significantly when the matter concerns the CIS countries. Uzbekistan's position is growing ever-stronger since it has positive balance with the majority of CIS countries.

Trade turnover with the CIS countries in compliance with inter-governmental agreements in 1994 made up US$ 1.8 billion or 63.0 per cent of overall trade turnover with the CIS countries. Hundreds of millions of dollars worth of essential goods, including oil, aircraft kerosene, rolled metal, wood and timber, spirits, food products, etc. were imported into the country. Uzbekistan in its turn exported output worth almost US$ 1 billion. Import-export balance with the CIS countries was more than US$ 142 million in favour of Uzbekistan.

The Republic's dependency on imports from the CIS states and foreign countries has significantly reduced on account of more than double increase of oil and oil products output, expansion of land area under farm crops and grain production growth. The independence the Republic's economy from external factors has also increased, something which enables to conduct more efficiently our domestic policy on the stabilization of economy and transition to market relations.

At the same time, Uzbekistan's relations with other states of the CIS, first of all with Russia, vividly demonstrate mutual advantages of cooperation and confirm the Republic's readiness to fruitfully cooperate with the CIS countries and strengthen and develop on a new foundation those multi-lateral economic, cultural, scientific and purely human relations which took shape in relations among our nations.

We attach paramount importance to the creation of favourable conditions for drawing on a broad scale foreign investments into our economy for development of foreign economic activity.

We have been guided by the following principles in carrying out measures for attracting foreign investments:

first, conducting a purposeful policy of further liberalization of external economic activity;

second, further improvement of legal, socio-economic and other conditions ensuring broad attraction of direct capital investments into the Republic's economy;

third, consistent conduct of the open doors policy in regard to those foreign investors which supply the Republic with high technologies and render assistance in the establishment of a modern structure of national economy;

fourth, concentration of resources in the top-priority directions ensuring the independence of the Republic and associated with the manufacture of competitive output.

A number of steps have been made in the field of institutional transformations on the establishment of organizations and agencies required for attraction of foreign investments. The National Insurance Company "Uzbekinvest" was established to cover political and commercial risks. "Uzbekinvest" and the National Bank of External Economic Activity jointly with the American financial group "ALG Inc." established joint insurance companies to cover political risks with the head-office in London and commercial risks — with the head-office in Tashkent. A group has started its operations in the country jointly with the EBRD on the elaboration of programmes to promote the preparation of feasibility study reports under investments projects for the purpose of the soonest utilization of US$ 60 million worth of investment loans allocated by the European Bank for reconstruction and development.

The investment promotion service, called upon to help foreign investors prepare investment proposals, was established under the Cabinet of Ministers within the framework of technical assistance programme of the United Nations Industrial Development Organization (UNIDO).

The Agency on Real Estate and Foreign Investments, called upon to promote attraction of foreign investments to the process of privatization, was established under the State Committee on Property and Foreign Investments.

A joint bank is expected to be established with the IFC and the Dutch "ABN-AMRO" Bank. The National Bank of External Economic Activity jointly with the IFC, EBRD and MayBank (Malaysia) established a joint leasing company.

The Republic introduced a system with a wide network of benefits for attraction of foreign investments, and foreign investors enjoy tax benefits. In compliance with Decree "On Measures for Intensification of Economic Reforms, Protection of Private Property and Promotion of Entrepreneurship", it is envisaged to grant tax holiday and exemption from payment of profit taxes and mandatory sale of currency to the Central Bank of the Republic of Uzbekistan for the term of five years from the date of registration to joint ventures specializing in the manufacture of consumer commodities.

The system of benefits and incentives currently in force envisages to:

— grant the enterprises irrespective of the form of ownership, the right to pay profit taxes at the rate reduced by half compared with taxes currently in force if the share of exportable commodities (work, services) make up not less than 30 per cent of their overall production scope;

— exempt from taxes for the term of five years projects included into the state investment programme of the Republic;

— provide unhindered and license-free export of output of own production;

— grant the right to duty free import of property for investing into joint ventures' Authorized capital stock, same relates to enterprises with hundred per cent foreign capital in the territory of the Republic of Uzbekistan;

— ensure free access of natural and legal personalities, including foreign legal entities to the process of privatization of state property, including sales of real estates;

— purchase on a competitive basis the right to long-term use and disposal of land for the implementation of investment projects.

The law on foreign investments established guarantees from nationalization and requisition for foreign investors. They are provided with guarantees to expatriate and amount of their profits and other amounts received as a result of their activity and the right to re-invest their income in the territory of the Republic and to open accounts in any currency without restrictions in the banks of the country.

There are reliable guarantees from changes in legislation, which envisage that those norms of legislation which were in force at the time of effecting investments shall be applicable in regard of foreign investors for 10 subsequent years.

Uzbekistan signed agreements on mutual protection of investments with Germany, Turkey, Egypt, Indonesia, Malaysia, Pakistan, Finland, Republic of Korea, USA and France. Similar agreements are expected to be signed with a number of other states.

The Government of Uzbekistan has concluded 32 major effective inter-governmental credit agreements with banks and companies of Canada, China, Turkey, the Netherlands, Germany and Switzerland amounting to about US$ 1.5 billion.

In 1994 agreements were entered into force with international financial institutions and foreign investors on providing the Republic with investment loans to the sum of US$ 640 million, of which about US$ 300 million are registered on credit lines for concrete projects. These include construction in progress of the International Trade-Exhibition Centre in Tashkent, sugar refinery in the Khorezm province and a gold extraction joint venture project with American "Newmont Mining Corporation" which is currently nearing completion.

The implementation of projects on the establishment of joint production lines started in Uzbekistan with the participation of foreign partners. Among them were "UzDAEWOOAvto" and "UzDAEWOOElectronics" (Republic of Korea), "UzItalMotor" Joint-Stock Association (Italy), "UzBAT" (Great Britain), Khorezm Automobile Production Association (jointly with "Mercedes-Bentz"— Germany), textile enterprises, etc. Modernization of telephone networks in the Republic has started jointly with German and South Korean companies.

Uzbekistan strives to take the place it deserves in the world community. We are open for the world and wish that the world was open for us.

1.8. ENSURANCE OF RELIABLE SOCIAL GUARANTEES IS AN IMPORTANT RESULT OF THE FIRST STAGE OF REFORM

Having taken to the implementation of radical economic reform, we arrived at one definite conclusion: the establishment of market economy is not an end in itself. **The final objective of all reforms — economic, democratic or political — is creation of decent conditions for human life and activity.**

In its turn, timely support of the most vulnerable and needy strata of the population serves as a guarantee of successful implementation of reform, and it is that social pillar which will not allow a turning back of the process of transformation and purification.

The experience of other countries prompts that the transition to market economy is not a smooth process, it is fraud with complications and social conflicts. Hence, the introduction of market mechanisms should objectively be complemented with strong preventive measures on social protection of the people.

At the earliest period of transition to market economy we were going along the road of anticipated social protection of the population. Guided by this principle, the government undertook energetic moves to hold control of the situation and consolidate the social sphere. This played a major role in preventing a sharp decline in the level of living standard of the population and served as a factor of maintaining tranquillity and stability in the Republic.

Today we have every ground to state that social policy elaborated and implemented at the initial stage of economic reform succeeded in the full realization of its tasks.

We have drawn an important lesson — the priorities of social policy, measures and mechanisms of rendering support to the population and its protection change with advancement toward market. Each concrete period of the initial stage of reform was substantiated by a corresponding system of measures on social protection, i.e. there was a distinctive mechanism of sub-adjustment of social protection moves for adaptation to changing economic conditions.

A wide range of means and methods of state regulation was used for this purpose. In particular, direct cash payments were effected in the form of regularly reconsidered amount of salaries, pensions, scholarships and various allowances and compensations and indirect payments in the form of benefits and subsidies. For instance, minimum salaries and pensions are not due to taxation. Enterprises' costs due to rendering social assistance to their employees were partially reimbursed on account of budget resources. Difference in prices on many types of consumer commodities and services were also reimbursed. At the same time, there was introduced a whole complex of additional social benefits: free breakfasts for primary school-children and students. Housing was turned over to many population groups for personal ownership for free. Certain privileges were introduced on some types of communal and public utility services, etc.

In spite of the complicated economic situation in conditions of limited material and financial means, there were always ways to find required resources for the solution of the most urgent, socially significant tasks. Expenses from social protection of the population made up about a third of the national budget for the entire duration of the first stage of reform. Thus, a mechanism of re-distribution was widely applied which enabled to mobilize necessary resources for the implementation of social measures.

The experience accumulated at the first stage of reform helped form a whole system of mutually-complementing moves directed toward maintaining all aspects of human life. All measures widely applied during complicated periods of making market relations are conventionally classified into individual major trends depending on their functional purpose and final effect. Moreover, there was permanent improvement of the forms and mechanism of rendering social support within these tendencies.

One of the main trends in the system of measures on social protection, covering practically all strata of the population and widely utilized in the course of the first stage of reform, **was and remains regular increase of the minimal and average levels of income in connection with price liberalization and growing rate of inflation.** We managed to elaborate our own approach to income indexation. As opposed to other countries, the process of income indexation in Uzbekistan was effected through one time centralized reconsideration of minimal salaries, pensions, scholarships and interest rates of population's deposits in savings banks.

In 1992—1994 minimal salary and minimal pensions were repeatedly raised and their amounts during this period increased 428 and 1230 times over respectively. Taking into account the social position of pensioners we invariably directed our efforts towards exceeding absolute amount of minimal pension over salary which matched the principles of social justice. Thus, currently the minimal salary is equal to 150 soums, while minimal old-age pension makes up 430 soums and disability pension is even higher.

Any raise of salary and other payments, as a rule, had a preventive nature and was tied up to the change of the price factor, which ensured maintenance of the population's solvency at certain level and prevented rapid fall in the living standard of the population.

Introduction of a Unified tariff netting in 1993 within the system of social protection of the population enabled through income indexation to directly tie-up payments to all categories of employees with a minimal salary. Thus, raising minimal salary meant automatic increase of average salary and monetary income of the population. Such a system ensured optimal proportions between the level of payment of various categories of employees, placed it in direct dependency on the quality and quantity of labour input preventing unsubstantiated differentiation in the levels of income and social stratification of the population.

The second major trend toward social protection of the population was adoption of measures on the protection of internal consumer market of the Republic and maintenance of consumption of essential food products and industrial good at certain level.

The need for the protection of the consumer market was predetermined by the more moderate, compared with our neighbours, policy of price liberalization. This was particularly important when Uzbekistan was in the rouble zone. We repeatedly faced the facts when food products in short supply —

flour, vegetable oil, sugar, etc. (many of which were purchased abroad for hard currency) in great quantities were taken out of the Republic.

We elaborated an integral system to prevent the collapse of the consumer market and introduced strict customs inspection and high customs taxes for the export of vital essentials. It also envisaged the introduction of one-time and, later, multiple-use coupons for the purchase of consumer commodities and organization of rationing of a limited range of essentials. This system fully justified itself. It not only enabled protection of the market but helped secure regular delivery of all vital food products and consumer commodities into the trade network and maintain the volume of their consumption.

With all the complexities of the transition period, this system secured reliable social guarantees for the entire population of the Republic in the part of consuming essential types of consumer commodities and services.

These moves were complemented in 1992—1993 by partial preservation of subsidies for bread and baked products, meat and meat products, milk, sugar, vegetable oil, soap, separate items of goods for children, public utilities and transport services, making them available for families with differing level of income. All this was of tremendous importance at the initial stage of reforms when in other countries of the former Soviet Union the impoverishment of the overwhelming majority of population became something routine. Our moves turned into a powerful factor for the people and instilled confidence in the necessity of implementation of reform.

Preparatory work was carried out in parallel on transition to a principally new system of protecting the interests of republican consumers. The essence of the matter lies in ensuring protective measures by the soonest possible equalization of domestic prices with the level of world prices corresponding to the increase of the incomes of the population. Great importance in the solution of this problem was given to the implementation of organizational and economic measures on the introduction of national currency into circulation and ensuring its internal convertibility.

The conclusion we have derived for ourselves was that only solid national currency supported by necessary commodity stock, preferably of the own production, and considerable currency reserves on account of broad export activity can reliably protect a domestic market and the interests of our nation.

Introduction of national currency made it possible by the end of the first stage of reform to completely abolish rationing of food products and introduce free prices. The elimination of the rationing system passed painlessly, without any break in the continuity of food supplies. Transition to free prices was not accompanied by any "shock" effects. This is an important result of the first stage of economic reform in Uzbekistan.

The third key trend in the implementation of active social policy at the initial stage was realization of decisive measures on social protection and support of low-income (needy) population groups. We were guided by the principle that it is a sacred duty of the state to protect socially vulnerable strata of the population — pensioners, invalids, families with many children and low income, unemployed, students and persons with fixed income.

Further material benefits including lower rent and lower pay for public utility services, immediate assignment of land under individual housing construction, etc. along with rise of salaries for the purpose of social protection and stimulation of labour were granted to teachers of all types of schools, tutors of orphanages, pre-school and adult education establishments, professorial and teaching staff and researchers of higher and special secondary educational institutions, creative and medical personnel.

Transition to market relations put single pensioners in need of nursing in jeopardy. Realizing the extent of their difficulties, a resolution was adopted to grant this category of pensioners exemption from payment of rent and utility services. They enjoyed the right to free medicine and essentials at the established norm and free travel in public transport. Special social assistance agencies were set up in the Republic in charge of rendering social and consumer services, nursing single pensioners and invalids at home.

Social protection of students and creation of necessary material conditions for studies is under permanent care of the state. Amount of grants and scholarships has repeatedly been raised to students of higher educational institutions, technical colleges and trade schools and post-graduate students.

Other forms of social protection of the youth have also been introduced. These included additional compensation to reimburse cost of nourishment, coverage of part of additional costs of school buffets and canteens on account of budget resources, compensation for rent, benefits for travel in public transport, etc. Conservation of national traditions prompted the introduction of benefits for the purchase of furniture, carpets and rugs for newlyweds.

These measures ensured reliable protection of the interests of the most needy and the most vulnerable strata of the population at the first stage of economic reform which provided an opportunity to prevent lumpenization of certain stratum of population and secure civil peace and accord.

The first stage of economic reform in Uzbekistan passed off under the sign of gradual transformation of the entire system of social protection of the population and its rationalized improvement. Low effective forms of social protection of the population were eliminated and transformed, and expenditures for social protection were adjusted to budget resource opportunities.

At the same time a deep analysis of the current system of social protection revealed its shortcomings and defects, wastefulness in the case of insufficient social return.

The former system of subsidies, allowances and benefits did not envisage concentration of resources on social support of population groups actually expecting social assistance, but it was oriented towards the entire population and insensitive to such factors as requirements of the needy. In other words, allowances were equally distributed among both the needy and well-to-do citizens. Moreover, with consideration of subsidies on essential commodities and real structure of consumption of these commodities and services by various categories of population it turned out that those who least needed social assistance enjoyed it to greater extent than those who needed it most.

There was a rather cumbersome system which tried to cover the entire population with low levels of actual social return and equalizing and redistributing mechanisms of implementation. Such form of support did not have any clear social foundation and was not distinctly addressed.

Suffice it to say that national budget had 30 various channels of providing social protection for the population and was quite vague in terms of concentration of resources and failed to substantially support namely those who needed it most.

It was vital to radically change the mentality of dependency established in the minds of the majority of the population which hampered the process of deepening economic reform.

The need for the implementation of a new social policy and improvement of mechanism of social protection of the population was objectively ripe. **In light of this, it was expedient to carry out gradual transition from the system of universal social protection to the system of reliable social guarantees and social support of the population.**

The principle of consistent domination of justice was laid down as the basis of establishing a renewed social policy. The essence of this principle is that the criteria which will have to be guided by in identifying those categories of the population who need state support; and the mechanisms to channel this support to them have to be, from their point of view simple enough, clear and just. Any display of subjectivism in identifying people in need of social guarantees and support and in determining a concrete type and amount of support will have to be completely excluded. The whole system should work to eliminate the psychology of equalization and dependency.

All this requires radical change in the existing methods of social assistance and sources of financing.

Social protection will have to be purposeful and concretely addressed. A differentiated approach to various strata of the population will have to become a specific feature of the new system of social protection. It has to clearly manifest its purposeful nature and is to be channelled toward those members of the society who need genuine material support of the state.

Assistance will have to be directed to families with low income and the disabled citizens. This will require the unification of the current types and forms of child allowances and benefits.

The funds of labour collectives and charity organizations and foundations along with available resources from government sources will have to be activity utilized for the solution of tasks in the sphere of social protection of the population and raising the level of their living standard.

The rights and responsibilities of local organs of administration, mayors and governors, neighbourhood committees will have to be substantially expanded. They should provide state guarantees for the most vulnerable strata of the population and, when necessary, take decisions and introduce additional benefits and allowances for securing social maintenance for local residents.

The most complicated and responsible task was precise identification of those channels and mechanisms which would enable to bring down the message of the state social maintenance programme to every one concrete addressee who need it most.

We have selected an approach of rejecting egalitarianism in the system of social protection of the population and finding our own path corresponding to moral and aethic values, way of

life and frame of mind of the nation which took shape throughout millennia in the East.

In this respect, the system of social protection of the population was radically changed. A completely new progressive system of social assistance was introduced which was a major result of the first stage of economic transformations in the field of social reform.

The new system was more unified with a much clearer orientation towards concrete consumers. Its distinctive feature is that its major consumers are the children — the future of our country, and families with low income. **Moreover, all allowances are paid and material assistance rendered only through families.** Thus, a key element of the modern system of social assistance is a family which fully meets the principles of universal humanism, national traditions and mentality of the nations and corresponds to the role the family plays in the system of social organization of civil society.

Along the preservation of a one-time payment at the birth of a child, the new system of social relief includes the following types of allowances and benefits.

First, child care allowance. Not only its amount **was increased, but the period of its payment was extended from one and a half years to two years.** Both working mothers and housewives now receive this allowance. Social justice was restored in regard to mothers and it became quite a great help for many families.

Second, a unified allowance to families with children under the age of 16 was introduced and all earlier paid child allowances and benefits abolished. The system of child allowances also was unified. Instead of more than 20 different child allowances, a unified allowance for all families with children entered into force in September 1994. The amount received is directly tied up to the structure of a recipient family. Moreover, the amount of a child allowance corresponds to the realities of the day and is directly tied up to any change in the minimum salary.

It has to be underlined that allowances to families with children under the age of 16 are paid out to all families irrespective of parents income and the income of the family on the whole. In other words, children under the age of 16 irrespective of various initial factors and reasons become direct objects of state assistance.

The state compensates part of family costs of rearing children and at the same time increases the level of their parents responsibility — maximum amount of allowance paid to a family with five children and more, was initially to 50 per cent and currently equals to 100 per cent of a minimum salary.

Third, Presidential Decree introduced material assistance namely to this category of families, starting from October 1994, and the state has been actively helping families with low income. The introduction of an allowance to families with low income is actually quite an unordinary step.

A characteristic feature of the family structure in Uzbekistan is that there is a good deal of multi-generational extended families living together and sharing the same household and common consolidated budget.

It was quite a problem under these conditions to select certain criterion for classifying families, relating them to the category of families with low income, and choosing means of its appraisal. The known methods of declaring profits turned out to be unacceptable in Uzbekistan. It would be quite unexpedient to choose a formal way of authorizing special agencies to provide families with allowances on the basis of presentation of references since it was fraud with display of subjectivism and deviation from the principle of supremacy of justice. This was predetermined by a number of reasons:

first, the majority of population resides in rural areas and makes income from household farming which is difficult to evaluate objectively;

second, such an approach would impel people to conceal their side-incomes and encourage dependency sentiments. We have not yet worked out methods of inspection of households which would take into consideration all sources of income.

A key to the solution of this problem was found in our own history when we researched sources of social organization of society in a powerful state which prospered in this land in ancient past. Centuries-old traditions of rendering assistance to the needy and poor formed in the depths and heart of the nations were also taken into consideration.

In Central Asia and, first of all, in Uzbekistan makhallya (neighbourhood) emerged in ancient times and is still preserved. It is a unique tradition of social self-organization. For Uzbeks makhallya means more than merely a community. **Specific principles of social and economic motivation of the native population, respect for social values, ethics of social relations which guarantee unconditional fulfillment of commitments and responsibilities before the society have been preserved thanks to makhallyas.**

The spirit of makhallya lives in the heart of every resident of our Republic.

This spirit, solidity and reliability of these ties among people and families through the current mechanism of self-organization of people in the form of makhallya was that key which enabled to open up the secrets of reviving the system of social justice in rendering assistance to the most needy.

The search for ways to organize an efficient system of social support was crowned by firm conviction that the most simple but efficient and open mechanism of implementing the programme of social assistance to the needy in Uzbekistan was the mechanism of rendering this assistance through makhallya. People with life-long experience capable of managing and arranging things live in makhallyas. The aksakals (elders) of makhallya elected on a democratic basis, their advisors and the most active members of the neighbourhoods, which the law provided the status of the organ of self-administration, know well the material and living conditions of every resident of makhallya and sources of every household's income.

Within the framework of the new system of social assistance, material support to families with low income is fixed by the assembly of makhallya residents. The novelty of approach to the mechanism of revealing taking account of and registration should particularly by noted because they are founded, on the one hand, on centuries-old traditions of the people to help their neighbours and display sympathy with their position, but, on the other hand, their intolerance of idlers and dependents. This results in our ability to distribute part of gross domestic product among the population which needs its most on the basis of decisions taken by people themselves without creating a clumsy bureaucratic structure.

Most importantly, this mechanism of rendering material assistance provided an opportunity to avoid humiliation of such families' dignity.

For the purpose of providing organs of self-administration with real resources for rendering assistance to the needy families, special funds were established in makhallyas determined by national and local budgets and voluntary donations made by enterprises and organizations, business structures and individuals. During the fourth quarter of 1994 alone, 360 million soums were assigned for these purposes from the state budget.

One of the most important results of the first stage of economic reform, leaning on tradition in our initially elaborated principles, Uzbekistan practically started the implementation of unique programme of addressed social protection of the population.

In conditions of the former command-administrative system when people were alienated from property, means of production and results of their labour, it failed to set up such a system of labour motivation which would involve the majority of people working efficiently with maximum realizations of their labour and creative potential.

Economic and social processes underway currently in this Republic radically change the structure of human activity motivation. The most active strata of the population is now being formed. Their economic interests are associated with aspiration to become proprietors or co-owners of property, to make profits, to have personal involvement in production management and to use their accumulated capital at their own will. The sense of proprietorship makes up the basis of their labour.

All hopes for the success of economic reform now rest and are linked primarily with the development of positive forms of labour motivation raising both labour and economic activeness of the population. A new system of labour motivations and incentives comes to life, which is reflected on the economic behaviour of people. The number of citizens, whose economic interests are associated with their preparedness to work at non-governmental enterprises or wishing to open their own businesses is growing day by day.

Transformation of the forms of ownership and formation of multi-structural economy is accomplished by gradual changes in the state of popular mind, values and objectives in the sphere of labour. A new system of labour motivations and incentives comes to life.

There is gradual transformation in the minds of the people, the ever-growing number of people start to realize that economic reform and transition to market relations is the only right way out of economic crisis and building a strong and independent state.

During the emergence of market relations, the sphere of education, public health service, science, culture and arts expect particular support since these are the fields on the development of which largely depend the moral atmosphere of the society and spiritual and physical condition of the people.

Measures on social protection of the population undertaken at the first stage eased transition to a new model of economic relations and promoted relaxation of psychological stress caused by the need of the soonest adaptation to swiftly changing economic situation, new conditions of life and living standard.

Transition to a new stage of economic reform will have to take into account the lessons derived from the previous stage and accumulated experience. **The main lesson is that the principles of domination of social justice, the addressed character of social support and their maximum return should be taken into full consideration in selecting criteria and mechanisms of social protection.** Problems of social protection of the population should be solved in close connection with problems of other social and economic complexes on the basis of national traditions and customs.

The state should come out as a guarantor of social stability and civic accord supporting the needy sections of the population and creating equal conditions and favourable environment for all capable people to build their prosperity and the prosperity of their family at their own risk.

1.9. SPIRITUAL AND MORAL REJUVENATION OF NATION IS A SOCIAL FOUNDATION OF ECONOMIC REFORM

Those concrete gains which found their embodiment in the spiritual sphere are undoubtedly the greatest achievements of the initial stage of renovation of society and economic reform. **Rejuvenation of spirituality and culture of the nation, regaining its genuine history and ethnic identity acquire. I would rather say, decisive significance for successful onward advancement along the road of renovation and progress of our society.**

Our policy of renovation and raising the level of ethnic-identity, political maturity and activeness of the population is based on a concrete foundation of reverting to our roots; on comprehension of the depth and grandeur of cultural and spiritual legacy of our great forefathers who contributed a tremendous share to the progress of the world culture; on bringing up a respectful attitude about our past, blessed national and religious traditions; and simultaneously on clear realization of the need to join in and assimilate with present-day world civilization, its values and spirituality.

Today when we live and work on building a just democratic society and a state with powerful economic potential, we cannot stay indifferent to the moral and spiritual basis of our transition to market economy. This is particularly urgent issue for the post-socialist countries where the principles of imaginary social equality, collectivist psychology and frame of mind had been ideologically imposed for decades. Market economy is guided by different, probably tougher and more demanding laws and rules. Prosperity of many depend, first and foremost, on themselves, and on their acclimation to new conditions and new relations. Everyone's destiny shall largely be determined by one's professionalism, moral principles and ability to adapt oneself to dynamically changing environment.

Transition to market economy is something like a maturity test. Frivolous spirituality and a cult of all-permissibility are absolutely intolerable under these circumstances. Hence the importance we attach to problems of spiritual and moral rejuvenation and purification. Only highly moral principles strongly rooted on noble spiritual and patriotic sentiments may serve as the basis for the establishment of truly civilized market relations and market mechanisms. Chaos and arbitrariness will otherwise settle in, as is the case, unfortunately, in a number of regions of the former Soviet Union and pseudo-market emerge, mixed on crime, corruption and moral degradation of people. This can in no way be allowed to happen. There can be no reference to conditions of the classical theory of "primary accumulation of capital".

It is not for this that we strived for independence and sovereignty and took to the road of radical transformations.

What are the principal moral lessons that we derived from the past experience of the first stage of economic reform?

First, life has convincingly proved the correctness of the road we had selected and the model of renovation and progress; it has proved that the implemented reform measures meet the interests of the people.

Second, independence of a state and its economy is not a blessing from the heaven, peace, stability and unity of a nation, common efforts and enterprising labour are the conditions for its achievement. Peace, stability and ethnic accord make people feel proud about our land irrespective of nationality, social origin or religious conviction.

Third, social market economy corresponds to high ideals of oriental Islamic philosophy, historical experience and mentality of our nation.

Fourth, our nation is a true master of its destiny, its wisdom and harmonious life are the guarantees of stability and changes for the better.

Fifth, and most important for us,— there are qualitative changes in the people's world outlook which match the requirements of contemporary realities, there are changes in regard to values and orientations in life. This is a distinctive feature of the first stage of reform.

Sixth, powerful opportunities of popular ethnic spirituality, morality and culture confirming the exclusive durability of the nation's mentality have been discovered thanks to reform and renovation of our society.

We are open for inter-relation and dialogue between various cultures, for their mutual enrichment relying heavily on the rich spiritual culture of the peoples of Uzbekistan, its unique historical past, invaluable philosophic and moral legacy.

Openness and traditions are the two components capable to further optimize the process of establishment of civilized market relations, development of science and technology and scientific-technical progress in general. They actuality make up the essence and originality of our own road of renovation and progress.

When we started the reform, we stemmed from certain principles whose authenticity now has been convincingly proved. Transition to market economy cannot help taking into account the objective conditions — way of life, psychology, traditions and culture of our nation.

The mentality of our nation is a major support of transformation of economy, state and the society on the basis of market relations. Spiritual independence and kindness, generosity and openness are inherent in our people. These wonderful qualities have passed the test of new economic life and conditions. Love for land, our Fatherland, and patriotism, the best features in the nature of the nation, cement the monolith of our spirituality.

The main source of our wealth, our independence and belief in the bright future is our native land. We love this blessed land, where the bodies of our great predecessors lie in peace; it warms us, feeds us and serves as an inexhaustible source of inspiration. We are bound to it in all our aspirations. In the time of joy and in the hour of sorrow we prostrate ourselves before it and it instills new strengths and new hopes. Our Land has a huge cultural legacy, in the territory of which many civilizations passed down their values from one generation to another, thus forming an uninterrupted time link and continuity of spiritual and cultural values.

Even with the current level of development of productive forces this land is able to feed all and even up to two and three times more people. People of all ethnic groups and convictions have understood that this is true. Only peace and stability are needed for that.

We, citizens of a free Uzbekistan, highly cherish the holy symbols of our independence — the State Coat-of-Arms, State Flag and the State Anthem. They serve as major symbols of spirituality and bring up the feeling of pride and infinite respect towards the Republic of Uzbekistan — the land of our forefathers. Our flag flutters proudly in the constellation of other flags of the UN member-states symbolizing the openness and equality of our relations with foreign countries.

Of paramount moral and educational significance was the institution of government awards — orders, medals and honorary titles — and the awarding of pioneers of independence and the heroic feats of our citizens. Patriotism is the chief "secret" of the unity of the people, reliable peace, stability and inter-ethnic accord in Uzbekistan.

To cherish, preserve and further develop this high sentiment and bring up our children to be worthy of a free and democratic Uzbekistan is the issue which has to make up the main trend of our activity in the sphere of spirituality.

Our nation is a possessor of such traditional levers of stability of the society as family and makhallya (neighbourhood) — the basic support of our mentality. Family and makhallya enable the people to deal efficiently with numerous problems of the current transition period and preserve the continuity of the good old and pragmatic present.

Nobody and nothing can be compared with the family in bringing up a pure and honest personality and in reviving one's mother-tongue. We value still more the significance of makhallya, neighbourliness, mutual-assistance in the best meaning of these words, as an unextinguishable center of spiritual and moral rejuvenation of nation, especially of the youth. The activity of the Republican "Makhallya" Foundation has found the broadest support of the population and public of Uzbekistan which deals with restoration of charming and good old holidays, traditions and rituals; rejuvenation of culture; rendering concrete assistance to the most needy families; and bringing up the feelings of humanism and charity.

The charity of the public, "sadaqa" coming from a generous heart has helped and will help single and needy old people, families with many children, invalids and students. A spring holiday "Navruz" brings joy and happiness to all people of Uzbekistan. We have preserved the most respectful attitude to the blessed memory of the fighters against fascism in the World War II and Victory Day. We are deeply respectful about war and labour veterans who devoted their lives to their Fatherland. We are deeply respectful of fathers, mothers and the elders.

Human and inter-ethnic friendship gains strength with every passing day. The measures carried out in this country at the state-wide level, celebration of anniversaries of prominent scholars, commanders, poets and writers acquire the form of a nation-wide holiday, make people feel better and more involved in the interests of the state. Our only interest is to secure peace and prosperity for people of all nationalities and beliefs residing in the Republic of Uzbekistan.

Vivid signs of high morality are major useful initiatives of non-governmental public foundations on the improvement of health of the coming generation, children and mothers, nature preservation and ecology in the broadest understanding.

Mention is to be made of such an outstanding result of renovation as the younger generation's aspiration to be worthy of the deeds of our great forefathers — geniuses of mankind. The growing attention displayed on the side of the state and the society to physical and moral upbringing of a new generation is a good sign of reform.

Trust in their reformer-state is firmly established in the mentality of the people of Uzbekistan. Every new step of the reform, every new draft of a new law and resolution of the government are interpreted from the position of humanness and benefit of the people. The people in this country fully trust and understand the need for the implementation of something unaccustomed to but essential for our progress.

Unity of transformation of all spheres of the country's life and spiritual and moral rejuvenation of the people — this principle has fully proved its viability. Oriental civilization and culture, which we are proud to be part of, have always been characterized by aspiration to prepare a nation both morally and spiritually for upcoming transformations.

Only a spiritually healthy and strong society may be ready for reform. Our nation manages to deal with the hardships of a transition period. The world can see the inexhaustible and moral grandeur of the entire population and all citizens of Uzbekistan. We are dealt with as the equals and are offerred mutually-beneficial cooperation.

Does a market economy have any good spiritual objective? Today there is every ground to provide a positive answer to this top important question. The ever-greater number of our people display initiative, sharp minds and skills in the sphere of efficient entrepreneurship. The ever-greater numbers of youth strives to master economic and production knowledge required for success in conditions of free and competitive labour. The native entrepreneurs strive not only to make profits but raise higher Uzbekistan's prestige in international economic ties.

The right of proprietorship and the sense of ownership has spread out wider and deeper among the people of the country and is causing major changes in their psychology and behaviour. Dependency and idling, although gradually and painfully, are passing away into oblivion. The concept of educational qualification aquires new meaning.

Revival of economically free labour — this is that moral condition which gradually comes back to our life. And it is being re-created by entrepreneurs, the people whose talents we have started to appreciate to their true value.

It is true, that during the transition period of market economy may arise various problems associated with theft, bribery, fraud and other violations of moral norms. But this is, primarily, the very product of spiritual poverty of individuals and their indifference to the destiny of the society.

We have revived the basic role of the Uzbek language in the life of the nation and the state and retained our respect to all languages spoken by the people living in Uzbekistan. Thus the dignity of the nation and the dignity of our independent state has been restored and consolidated. Our country will enter the 21st century, which is going to be a century of information technologies, with a solid foundation for the most dynamic development of all-round contacts in the sphere of science, technology, economy as well as in the field of education, culture and more open human inter-relations.

We are honouring the creative heritage and exploits of Amir Temur, Mirzo Ulughbek, Mukhammad Zahiriddin Babur, Imam al-Bukhari, al-Termezi, Bahauddin Naqshbandi, Hoji Akhmad Yassavi and other great forefathers of the Uzbek people and outstanding personalities in the history of civilized mankind. Magnificent monuments have been erected in their honour, palaces, madrassahs and mausoleums restored, squares and streets of many towns and settlements given their names. Our ancient towns and cities have regained their significance as centers of world culture and host major scientific conferences and symposia welcoming prominent scholars both from the East and the West.

We return our own history both to ourselves and to the rest of the world. This is an outstanding result of reform.

Thanks to an inalienable combination of state independence and devotion to progress and democracy, our country has been able to win much respect in the world culture. In recognition of our nation's contribution to the civilization of mankind were celebrations of the 600th birth anniversary of an outstanding astronomer and statesman Muhammad Taraghai Ulughbek at the decision of UNESCO in Paris.

A decision on the establishment of a public Center of spirituality and enlightenment "Ma'naviyat va Ma'rifat" seems to be a significant event in consideration of modern tasks and perspectives of Uzbekistan's development. Its branches started their spiritual and enlightenment activity in the makhallyas, labour collectives, educational institutions, and among urban and rural residents. Book-printing and means of mass media have been preserved and supported by the government. The first attractive issues of the magazine "Tafakkur" (Thought) have already come off the press.

Progressive intelligentcia, scientists, writers, workers of art and culture, clergymen are staunch supporters of the policy of reform. Thanks to this, our spiritual and intellectual potential ha incomparably strengthened. A nation-wide intellectual and cultural space is being established in this country. As a powerful magnet due to its humanism, grandeur, optimism and faith, it attracts all who live in our land and build our common home irrespective of race, nationality, religious and political convictions.

Ethnic accord for the Uzbek people is the most important condition of inter-ethnic accord in our country which welcomed representatives of more than 130 nationalities as its own people. There are plenty of examples which prove that sovereignty, peace and stability in our country is a common weal not only for Uzbeks but for all other nations living in this land. More and more people acquire the right to get education in their own language and bring up their children in their national spirit. National cultural centers are engaged in the noble mission of cultural and spiritual rejuvenation. At the same time they help consolidate the sense of nation-wide patriotism in Uzbekistan.

Law and economics provide equal opportunities for all, while humanness, kindness, charity and mutual tolerance, respect and compassion peculiar to Uzbeks —"Uzbekness" known to everyone throughout centuries forms the atmosphere of benevolence and confidence.

Oriental philosophy holds the place it deserves in our life along with our aspirations to common human values. We have restored the rights of great cultural values of Islam, and the deeper our soul absorbs these values, the spiritually wealthier and morally purer becomes life of the nation.

There is a rise of the spiritual role of our forefathers' religion — Islam — in the life of man and his family. Morality and charity harmoniously combines secularism of our state and freedom of conscience.

The society of Uzbekistan is united around the ideals of state independence and economic prosperity. Peace, harmony, stability and transformations in the interests of man reign in this country. Spiritual and cultural needs of the population have grown up in gigantic proportions as well as the need for education and understanding of fundamentals of economics. Our people have been able to protect their spiritual freedom, faith and dignity and are ready for the accomplishment of greater deeds for the sake of a better future.

A number of prospective conditions have been established in the course of the first stage of transformations which are still expected to reveal themselves at the new stage of reform. These large-scale phenomena include the emerging nation-wide ideology of national independence. We have drawn up an important conclusion that not a single ideology should raise to the level of state ideology.

Ideology of national independence, based on age-old traditions, customs, language and the spirit of our nation, in close combination with general human values should serve the task of bringing to the hearts and minds of the people confidence in the future, bring up love for Fatherland, love of fellow-men, benevolence, courage and tolerance, feeling of justice and aspiration for knowledge and enlightenment. It is called upon to promote spiritual rapprochement among citizens of the state on the road to great objective.

The true essence of the new ideology is to bring up independently thinking people free from prejudices of the past.

The society has derived the following conclusion from the first stage of reform: civilized market economy addressed to people is to be built on a solid foundation of spirituality, morality and culture. These are life-giving sources of peace, stability and inter-ethnic accord in Uzbekistan. They are our most treasured wealth. We have well understood how important it is to keep and multiply this spiritual treasure and communicate it to the possibly greater number of people.

One of philosophers said that spirituality is a road leading to humanness. Along this road, the road of goodness and humanness independent Uzbekistan keeps going towards its future.

1.10. SECURING ECONOMIC AND SOCIO-POLITICAL INDEPENDENCE IS THE MAIN RESULT OF THE FIRST STAGE OF REFORM

Consistent implementation of economic reform has produced tangible results in the transformation of economy, liberalization and openness to the world community. Genuine conditions have been established for transition to market mechanisms of management.

Purposeful and gradual advancement along the road of reform provided an opportunity to form the basis of multi-structural economy, market infrastructure and currency market as well as other major elements of making of a socially-oriented market economy. This is, no doubt, the most important result of the first stage of reform. But not only this.

The tasks of overcoming economic crisis and achievement of economic and financial stability were given priority in determining the objectives of the intial stage of reform. We have every reason to state that on the whole this task was successfully solved. We managed to stop the expanding decline in economy and decreasing production volume in the leading structurally-decisive sectors and to stabilize inflation rate and prevent sharp decrease in the living standard of the population.

It has to be openly admitted that newly independent Uzbekistan and its people lived through hard and serious trials later in 1991 and 1992. We passed the test of political and statehood maturity, the test of ability to independently decide our own destiny and protect our independence and freedom.

With the collapse of the ex-USSR and destruction of economic links the Republic turned out to be squeezed in the grip of the most severe deficit of financial and strategically vital raw resources. Our biggest enterprises, dependent on deliveries from other regions and countries, found themselves on the brink of a standstill. The situation was further deteriorated by the low starting level of the population's material level, high level of dependency from supplies of major food products, medicine and deep structural and price disproportions.

Elaborating our own strategy of economic reform and starting its realization, we objectively assessed that compared to Russia, Ukraine, Belarus, to say nothing of the Baltic state we were certainly in unfavourable starting conditions. This did not deviate us from our firm conviction about the successful implementation of economic reform. On the contrary, it helped mobilize our efforts and internal opportunities and prompted us to seek the most optimal ways for the solution of the most acute social and economic problems.

Enough time has passed since then to evaluate the correctness of strategies chosen by each country and the principles of implementation of reform and its course.

There were no obvious major difference at first glance. All the CIS countries have to switch from centralized planned system with administrative-command principles of management to market economy. All countries adopted laws directed towards shaping market relations, established corresponding institutional structures, elaborated market mechanisms of economic regulation and carried out privatization of state property. However, the results of the first stage of reform turned out to be different.

What is the reason for that?

First and foremost, is the choice of approaches and principles of reforming. Many of the CIS states, following the recommendations of international economic and financial organizations placed the questions of the most expedient liberalization of prices and foreign trade in the center of their economic policy in transition of market relations.

And the solution of growing problems of inflation was related in practice with a rather tough monetary and financial policy. That is, purely monetary methods of macro-economic regulation were applied. These methods are well-known — reduction of budget deficit, credit emission, stabilization of national currency rate on account of currency intervention on the side of Central Banks at inter-bank currency auctions. A systematic policy of sequestration of state expenditures for the purpose of bringing them to balance with incoming revenues is conducted to maitain acceptable budget deficit.

It was hoped that the well-tested methods of monetary policy in industrialized countries would produce the same results in the economies of the CIS countries. However, the absence of market mechanisms of regulation which make the monetary policy sufficiently effective in advanced countries were completely ignored.

With the consideration of these factors were advanced ambitious programmes of macro-economic stabilization which envisaged reduction of inflation level down to 1-3 per cent and sharp curtailment of budget deficit. But these were not destined to be implemented. Thus, the level of inflation in Russia by the end of 1994 sharply increased and exceeded 16 per cent, while the budget deficit equalled 13 per cent of the gross domestic product; the rouble keeps falling. In Kyrghyzstan industry, agriculture and material well-being of the people were sacrificed to stabilize national currency. All this is an eloquent proof of the failure to achieve final objectives.

The experiences of a number of CIS countries has it that a tough monetary-credit policy at the initial stage of reform may produce in itself the sole effect — sharp decline in production.

In our view, the fall in the volume of production, particularly in the basic sectors of industry should be recognized as the most alarming manifestation of crisis in the national economy of the CIS countries. Thus, in Russia the gross domestic product decreased by 39 per cent, in Ukraine — by 40 per cent, in Kazakhstan — by 43 and Kyrghyzstan — by 48 per cent. The volume of industrial production fell down by 44 per cent in Russia, 38 per cent in Ukraine, 48 per cent in Kazakhstan and 58 per cent in Kyrghyzstan. A particularly difficult situation emerged in science-intensive sectors which make up the basis of economic growth. Industrial production of consumer commodities was radically reduced. There is an obvious tendency of de-industrialization of these countries. Also high are the rates of decline in agriculture and capital construction.

Thus, there is a noticeable acceleration of destruction of material, social and spiritual foundations in ensuring the supplies of essentials for the population of these countries. Quite a number of them are unable to secure even simple reproduction, which brings about a fall in production efficiency, stoppage of enterprises and greater level of unemployment. Motivation of labour and traditional system of human relations are also subject to deformation and destruction.

Numerous reasons for deepening crisis are cited today. Among the major reasons are the following ones:

First, according to evaluation of the architects of reforms, these are the consequences of insufficient preparation for transition to market, unexpected, poorly considered and crumbling price liberalization, imposed by international experts, in the monopolistic state economy.

Liberalization turned out to be cut off from other trends of economic reform — structural changes, institutional transformations, privatization processes, and most importantly, from efficient mechanisms of social protection of the population.

Second, the monetary macro-economic policy did not have adequate mechanisms of realization at micro-level. Stress was made on limiting demand and not on expansion of supply. The result was growth of non-payments and collapse of production. Moreover, one point missed consideration: curtailment of inflation alone not yet an indication of improvement in the economy.

Third, an in-depth reason of prolonged and growing production decline, something admitted by the leaders of perestroika, was the weakening of state influence on economic processes and an impermissibly low level of state and labour discipline at all levels and in all spheres of economic activity.

Fourth, practically no attention was paid to undertake efficient measures on rendering protection and social support to the population. That meant the removal of social support from under reform. Moreover, the utilization of unnatural methods of artificial bridling of inflation, sometimes on the brink of violation of human rights (long delays with the payment of salaries, pensions, etc.) may invariably lead to social consequences and social explosion.

In contradistinction to a number of Commonwealth countries there was no production collapse or sharp decrease in the living standard of the population. We managed to avoid economic and political chaos which overwhelmed the other regions of the former Soviet Union after its disintegration. Moreover, the Republic maintained socio-political and socio-economic stability and consolidated all social forces in support of its policy.

This is ensured on account of mutually-coordinated economic and social policy, which enabled us to prevent destabilization of economy and the society, preserve state management of economy and reliably protect the interests of the people during complicated transition period.

Gradual, step-by-step advancement along the chosen course of reform, perfection of state regulation of market relations, liberalization of economy and social support of the population enabled us to a certain extent to avoid the deterioration of macro-economic indicators.

In the field of macro-economic stability, there had been a certain tendency towards slowing down the rates of production while there was also certain growth on some positions. Gross domestic product made up 96.5 per cent in 1994 while material national income equalled 92.6 per cent.

Decrease in gross domestic product was mainly the result of structural shifts and production decline because of reduction in the level of demand on output in some industries — the industry of building materials, chemical, metallurgical, tractor and farm machine building industries, in civil engineering, etc.

An insignificant recession in production may be classified as a cyclic one, which makes up, as a rule, from 5 to 15 per cent and does not have any considerable destructive effect. On the contrary, such recession is inevitable since it is linked, in the first place, with diversification of production structure and the formation of a new economic mechanism.

In 1994 the volume of industrial output in the Republic comprised 101 per cent compared with the previous year of 1993. Certain positive structural shifts in the industry could clearly be identified. The share of industries ensuring fuel and power independence of the Republic, manufacturing the end products and oriented towards satisfying the needs of the population, increased on account of sustained development of leading base sectors of economy. The share of end consumption output in the overall production volume went up to 35.2 per cent.

There is steady decline in the production of power resources in the countries of the CIS. For example, oil extraction in Russia shrank by 10 per cent in 1994 alone, in Kazakhstan — by 12 per cent; gas extraction in Russia went down by 2 per cent, in Turkmenistan — by 45 per cent. These indicators have been growing in Uzbekistan: extraction of oil and gas condensate has doubled in the Republic in recent years, in 1994 alone — by 40 per cent and gas production increased by 5 per cent during the same year.

We used to import four million tonnes of oil in the past. The volume of purchases decreased with every passing year on account of our own production of oil in this country. In 1995 we will buy 750 thousand tonnes of oil on the side. Similarly we expect to achieve grain independence within the coming two-three years. This is not solely economic, but also is a major political task.

Despite cancellation of in-flow of resources from the All-Union budget and reduction of the real volume of production we managed to stabilize the financial situation, limit real state expenditures and prevent the growth of state budget deficit, which required the conduct of a tough financial and tax policy.

For several years now the state budget deficit remains at the level of lower that 4 per cent from gross domestic product. Financing on account of budget was effected on a monthly basis and only within the limits of incoming resources.

Rates of re-financing were increased from 40 up to 225 per cent; reserve requirements of banks went up 10-13 per cent; credit and cash emission were drastically limited.

The introduction of regulated salary fund depending on the growth of physical volumes of production and the raising of deposit rates on personal accounts of the population resulted in slowing down the dynamics of bulk money the increment of which during 1994 alone went down 1.7 times over.

The implementation of the anti-emission programme considerably reduced the level of cash settlement —from 30 per cent on the average in the first half of 1994 down to 17 per cent by the early 1995. Additional means and resources were looked for to fill in domestic consumer market, stabilize the operation of leading industries and enterprises and adapt them to market conditions within the shorest possible time.

The general economic situation during the initial stage of reform took shape under the active impact of price liberalization. By the end of 1994 the process of transition to free market prices was on the whole completed. Free contract prices were established practically on all types of industrial output, on food and non-food products. All factors which could cause hidden inflation were removed in 1995.

The adoption of effective anti-inflation measures enabled us to cut down by half the average monthly inflation rate in the second half of 1994, that is from 31.7 per cent down to 15.1 per cent while money circulation rate trebled. The introduction of national currency into circulation in the second half of the year had a strong impact on the reduction of the inflation level.

Reduction of the inflation level in conditions of price liberalization is a visible and tangible result of conducted economic policy. One of the most important tasks for the feasible future is to consolidate the achieved success in fighting inflation. This is particularly essential with consideration of repeated price rises.

A decisive role in achieving relative economic stability in Uzbekistan belongs to weighted regulating policy of the state which became the chief reformer of institutional and system transformations.

Today many of the CIS states consider more closely our road of renovation and progress and study deeper the mechanism of implementation of reform in close connection with strong emphasis on social protection of the population. Both Belarus and Ukraine would not mind to make wide use of our experience accumulated in the course of reform.

At the same time the past stage taught us some lessons; their consideration is vital for subsequent advancement toward market economy.

1. Global rejection of state regulation of economy in conditions of still emerging self-regulation under the impact of demand and supply and free competition of consumer manufacturers with limited opportunities in external economic relations promotes considerable rise in prices and inflation.

2. Rejection of any form of state regulation of population incomes brings them to inadequately high level under economic conditions of transition period; these incomes are in disproportion with commodity coverage — all this causes still higher inflation rate.

3. Tough tax policy, first and foremost in regard to output manufacturers, does not secure deficit-free state budget, but at the same time reduced investment opportunities of commodity producers themselves, coupled with the continued inflation process compels manufacturers to use the greater part of their net produce for consumption.

4. Production structures still remain highly monopolized and restrain the shaping of a competitive environment.

5. Stability in economy is unimaginable without the establishment and development of mutually-beneficial external economic relations and production cooperation with foreign partners.

6. Extremely important is support of top-priority trends in the development of economy, particularly in base industries, attracting for these purposes both internal and foreign investment resources.

An important lesson of the first stage was comprehension of the need for coordinated actions of all central economic agencies with constant examination of the results of decisions and operative introduction of respective corrections of mechanisms for achieving basic priorities of economic reform.

Achievement of economic stability in combination with measures on social protection of the population enabled us to secure stable sociopolitical situation in the Republic.

At the initial stage of radical transformations, we managed to prevent a sharp decline in the consumption of essential food products and non-food commodities, mass unemployment; secure maintenance and operation of branches of social sphere — health services, education, science and culture.

On the basis of objectively shaped conditions, and ethnic and psychological stereotypes, special attention was attached to problems of food supplies, creation of favourable conditions for self-employment of rural residents at their individual land holdings and fast-expanding dekhkan (farming) sector.

This made possible the prevention of sharp social stratification of society, which would inevitably cause social tension and, as a consequence, political crises similar to those in Russia, Ukraine and Belarus.

On the other hand, social conditions were established for consistent implementation of reform.

Social support was implemented in combination with political moves on the establishment and consolidation of Uzbekistan's independence, revival of ethnic identity, preservation and development of mother-tongue and national traditions, securing social rights and guarantees to representatives of other ethnic groups and the development of spirituality of the society.

The principal achievement of the first and initial stage of establishment and development of independent Uzbekistan is maintenance of socio-

political stability, civic peace and inter-ethnic accord in our multi-national society.

The political peculiarity of independent Uzbekistan is revealed in its stability, constructive inter-relation between various political movements, and the absence of delimitation into various confronting political groupings by class, social or religious indications. An established opinion that true democracy emerges out of political confrontation has a startling effect. Worldly wisdom has it that a sick mother cannot bear a healthy child.

The Republic introduces a socio-political system which meets the requirements of advanced international and our internal experience, mentality of the people and universally recognized human rights. We fully renounce the totalitarian one-party system and state monopoly on social policy.

A reformer-state promotes the diversity of the country's political life. The first steps have been made on the road to a political multi-party system, fixed in the Fundamental Law — Constitution, on the basis of which the first elections were held into the highest organ or power — Oliy Majlis (Supreme Assembly).

Our society has successfully coped with another complicated task of democratic upbuilding: we stood up on a new higher level of legal and civic maturity and socio-political stability.

We should also keep in mind that for centuries our people have elaborated our own mechanisms of display of solidarity and conducting public opinion polls through makhallya (neighbourhood) gatherings and councils of elders. Makhallyas and veterans are the most influential force of a healthy public opinion. The use of rights and freedoms provided for by law to local self-administration of citizens has a favourable impact on consolidation of stability, coordination of moves undertaken by the state and the needs and opinion of the people.

An important political lesson has been derived from the past period. The larger the number of economically independent citizens, the more solid are conditions for lawful democracy and mature political relations.

Stability, peace, and accord — this is the foundation on which we are erecting a new building of our statehood. This is a window into our bright morrow.

The experience of the first years of Uzbekistan's independence prove that:

First, the deeper, the more complicated and larger in scale are the transformations implemented in the society, the more solid are stability, peace and accord among its members. Solidarity and not confrontation is to prevail in relations among people irrespective of their ethnic origin, religious and political convictions. Good-neighbourliness and mutual respect: it is an age-old truth inherited from our fathers and grandfathers which makes the essence of national character and spiritual mentality of our people — this is the first principle and guarantee of our society's well-being.

Second, any, even the biggest changes in politics, economics and social sphere should be of constructive nature. Most important is to be able to preserve and not to destroy all that which was accumulated through hard work, by the sweat and the blood of the previous generations. No social building can be improved if it's repeatedly shaken to its foundation.

Third, people expect and demand from organs of administration and management a painstaking daily work on the elaboration of legal norms opening up the road to market transformations, on persistent implementation of adopted decisions, on real solution of concrete practical tasks for the purpose of improvement of living conditions of the population, and on advancement of the Republic along the road of national and social progress. These are what people expect from local organs of administration and management — not political declarations, not eloquent phrases or slogans and not exhortations about prosperous future. There can be no higher merit than to justify this trust. There can be no more evil than to betray this trust.

And, **fourth,** it is vital to protect people and the society from extremists and political adventurists and prevent any attempt to sow enmity, discord and confrontation. In peace, accord and through mutual assistance we shall be able to overcome all hardships.

Peace, tranquillity, and accord are life-giving source, instilling hope and confidence in the morrow and in the bright and prosperous future for those living today, their children and descendants. Having peace and stability is a key to integration with the world community. Only those countries and nations who accept and share generally-recognized values of humanism, kindness and sincerity can be closely associated with and understood by all nations of the world and be accepted into the world community. Only with them will building equitable mutually advantageous cooperation be possible.

Only in conditions of peace and tranquillity will it be possible to persistently and intelligently, stage by stage re-structure the society and the whole economy.

The integrity of socio-political and economic aspects of reform is a major achievement of our road of renovation and progress, an embodiment of our own model of transition to a market economy. Its strategic outcome is the current socio-political and economic stability in Uzbekistan.

Part 2

TASKS AND PRIORITIES
OF THE SECOND STAGE OF ECONOMIC
REFORM

While giving the realistic estimation of the situation in the Republic, we can rightfully ascertain that Uzbekistan has entered the qualitatively new stage of its state, political and economic building.

The results of the initial stage of transformations convincingly testify that the first visible steps have been taken to establish political and state systems which meet the interests, national traditions and mentality of the multinational people of Uzbekistan.

In the conditions of social and political stability, civil and inter-ethnic accord has been laid the basis of new economic relations, particularly the relations of ownership which meet the requirements of the market economy. The non-state, private sector of economy is gaining strength and becomes firmly established. Crucial changes have taken place in the structure and mechanisms of management. They gave the enterprises the freedom of economic management, promoted the development of initiative and entrepreneurship.

The Republic of Uzbekistan has considerably advanced towards the solution of the problems connected with overcoming the economic crisis, recession, improvement of structural deformations in the economy. There have been created economic and institutional prerequisites and the new national currency —"soum"— has been introduced. Radical improvements have been introduced into the financial, taxation and monetary systems, the effective measures have been taken to regulate emission and to reduce the level of inflation. The fundamentally new system of social protection has been established that effectively protected interests of the population in the transition period, particularly of the socially vulnerable groups and families with children and prevented the unemployment growth.

The radical changes in the economy and social sphere allowed to create sound starting conditions for transition to the next, qualitatively new stage of development.

We have repeatedly pointed out that the scale and depth of the problems which are to be achieved during the transition period, predetermine the necessity of the gradual implementation of the process of reform. We have elaborated the strategy of reform — the general ideology of transformation of the economy and transition to market relations. Besides, each stage is characterized by its own strategic goals and priorities, formation of its specific targets that require appropriate forms and methods of implementation of economic policy, specific levers and facilities of its realization.

That is the distinctive feature of our way of transition to the market when the consistent transition to new stage, to a new phase of the development is carried out after the previous stage is completed and necessary prerequisites created. The duration of each stage is determined not by time limits, they may vary greatly, but it depends rather on the range of problems to be solved.

Today the Republic has consistently entered the next stage of transformation of the society. The second stage is the natural period resulting from our general strategy, the period of advancing along the road of progress and renovation. This is the period when the process of reformation widely involves all branches of economic and social life of our society. This is the period of more profound system and institutional transformations, formation of mature market relations and stratum of real owners of the means of production.

The second stage is called up onto finish the formation of market structures, it encourages the further improvement of taxation, financial and monetary policies, liberalization of all types of external economic activities. It is aimed at strengthening of the economic system of our young state, achievement of economic independence and ensuring stability of circulation and internal convertibility of the national currency. This is the period of creation of sustainable base for activization at the next stages of investment activites, implementation of deep structural transformations and ensuring on this basis economic growth and wide integration into the world economic system, strengthening of its holds in it.

Proceeding from the targets of the second stage of economic reform the main tasks to focus our efforts and resources on are the following.

The first, and perhaps the main task is to finalize the efforts commenced in the field of privatization of the state property.

Its essence is in the accelaration of assignation of property to the actual owners, to inspire the feeling of a real proprietor in them.

It is necessary to significantly expand the non-state sector share in the public production through the privatization of the state property, active support for promotion of the small private enterprises establishment business activities, promotion of the small private enterprises establishment.

The second important task of the present period of reform is to overcome the recession and to ensure the macro-economic stabilization, to achieve the economic and financial stability of enterprises and of the state as a whole.

This presupposes the creation of meaningful conditions for stabilization and increase of the output, stimulation of production activities. It is necessary to clearly understand that it would be impossible to implement the actual advance towards the civilized market, to protect independence economically, to create reliable social guarantees and decent life for the many-millioned population of Uzbekistan without reconstructing its own production and rise in economy.

The third important task is to further strengthen the national currency — soum. The important priority of the economic as well as of social reforms being carried out in our country lies in strengthening our own currency which serves as a specific indicator of the stability of the economy, as a barometer of the successful implementation of the transformations contemplated. There is no sound economy without strong and authoritative national currency.

It is necessary to strive for its convertibility in every way possible. This can be achieved through the effective antiinflation measures, building up domestic production of the consumer goods and saturation of our domestic market with them, strengthening foreign exchange reserves through expansion of the export activities of enterprises.

The fourth strategic task is to crucially change the structure of our economy, to shift from the orientation to raw materials on the production of finished goods, to make their quality and competitiveness meet the world with the world market requirements.

For all that the structural transformations, in the first instance, are to be aimed at ensuring economic independence in the development of such key sectors for the Republic as fuel and energy and grain producing complexes, at the outstripping growth of the priority for the country branches of production, which are based on the rich natural, mineral labour resources and which in the future guarantee for Uzbekistan the stable hold in the international and interstate division of labour, in the world market. The real independence cannot be obtained without crucial transformation of the economic structure.

Another urgent task is to expand the production of goods according to the world standards, to increase their competitiveness. The accomplishment of this task requires to supply the enterprises with updated technology, advanced equipment including compact equipment for small and medium enterprises. While attaching great importance to this problem, the first session of the Oliy Majlis put forward the idea of necessity to elaborate a concept and national programme for introduction of productions consuming small technologies which would enable to saturate domestic market over a short period of time. Development such programme and launching it is the priority of the second stage of economic reform.

We have to clearly realize that we will not be able to ensure the development of our state and to reach the well-being without having enterprises retooled with updated technologies and equipment, promoting the improvement of professional skills of those working and formation of the national labour environment, without introduction of advanced, world level methods of organization of production management, promotion of the development of competitive products, without finding markets for these products.

The second stage should follow up the earlier undertaken efforts aimed at strengthening social protection of poor population, at offering them relevant assistance. This is our constant priority. In the course of reform it is necessary to ensure the people the stipulated by the Constitution equal social guarantees and possibilities in the realization of their labour and intellectual potential, in receiving fair wages for their labour. The initiative and enterprise should be encouraged in all possible ways. It is necessary to intensify the process of transition to the system of direct social support of the population. It is no less important to help some individuals to get rid of their parasitical attitude as soon as possible. All these in the long run will envision the necessity to change the attitude of the people, to shape up the psychology of market relations.

We all should understand well that life raises the situation and changes — therefore we should look for new approaches and non-standard solutions. This is the essence and the requirement of the second stage of the economic reform.

2.1. EXTENSION OF THE PRIVATIZATION PROCESS AND FORMATION OF THE COMPETITIVE ENVIRONMENT IS THE KEY TASK OF THE NEW STAGE OF ECONOMIC REFORM

Proceeding from the strategic goals of the economic transformation, the second stage will continue the commenced efforts aimed at privatization of the state property and formation of the multi-sectorial, socially oriented economy. This is the priority of the second stage. We have set ourselves the task to finish the primary privatization of the state property, to form the stratum of actual owners, to allot them with real property, to crucially change the structure of public production for the dominating non-state sector.

At the same time the privatization process should not be considered as the end in itself of economic reforms. Privatization is not a panacea from all the vices in the economy and social sphere inherited by us from the totalitarian and completely state-controlled system. Therefore, we should not view the very process of privatization as a final goal and consider that its major result should be the number of enterprises and the period over which they have changed their form of property. I would call it a simplified primitive approach.

Substitution of the complicated process of privatization which crucially changes the whole system of economic relations, bears the tremendous, reformatory supply, for the mere campaign of mere denationalization does not promote the deepening of reform, but rather discredits the very concept of economic advantage of the production based on private property and personal motivation of labour. The experience of other countries provides us with a number of examples when mass privatization has practically brought no desired results for the revival of the economy. Moreover, without appropriate preparation, without creating effective mechanism of support for enterprises, it aggrivated the economic crisis, drove many enterprises to the verge of bankruptcy, increased unemployment as well as intensified stratification of population by their income and social status. No wonder that such privatization was not welcomed by the majority of the working people and became the subject of corrupt, criminal bargain.

We should clearly realize that privatization is not the result but one of the directions, one of the most important ways of implementation of the economic reform. Two key tasks are to be solved as the result of privatization.

First, the property which is available with us shall be obtained its real owner. The concept of the economic reforms being carried out is to transfer the property to the hands of real masters, to provide them with wide opportunities for the entrepreneurship activities.

I would like to stress that the question is not in the mechanical replacement of the state owner by the collective, joint stock or private owner. The question is that the property should be allocated to the owner who could zealously master this wealth.

This is the owner who would not squander the property obtained and turn it into the source of personal enrichment, but would rather increase this property, retool it and update it, and to use it for manufacturing competitive products. This is the owner who could organize the production in such a way that it would provide jobs for the disengaged population, bring profit to the owner himself as well as to the workers and the state.

This could be reached only in case the state property is transferred to the new owner not free of charge but through its redemption. It is a common knowledge, that the thing has no price shall not be not really valued and protected. Therefore, we shall continue to adhere to the principle of privatization on the basis of payment to compensate for the expenses connected with creation of this property. To achieve this we will more widely apply such privatization techniques as the establishment of joint-stock companies, sale of the units on tender basis and through auctions.

What advantages does the feeling of a real owner actually give? First of all, the character of economic relations crucially changes. There disappears the necessity for command and administrative compulsion for development and expansion of production. The actual producer gets set free, liberated from the chains of command dictates. Private business, command and administrative principle are incompatible. The producer is prompted by the qualitatively new motives and incentives, by the real awareness of the results of his activities and growth of his economic responsibility.

Providing to be the proprietor, the owner of the property, the master of his labour and the products produced, an individual liberates his internal energy, intellectual and creative potential, organizational abilities, fills himself with the initiative and enterprise. The enterprise ruled by the real master always has clear and precise prospects for development, higher effectiveness of production, higher profits and higher wages for workers. The more real and well-off owners we have, the sooner we create economic conditions providing high wages for all those wishing, the richer our Republic becomes.

The second important task to be solved in the course of privatization is the establishment of multi-sector economy and encouraging competitive environment.

Role of privatization in the formation of competitive environment is versatile. First of all, destruction of state monopoly and creation of many enterprises involved in similar activities or producing similar products or services is based on various forms of property — state, collective, joint-stock, private and other. Privatization allows to eliminate current monopoly of some enterprises and whole spheres of activities, create possibilities for development of free economy and competitive environment. There appears economic competitiveness with the efficiency of production, with the markets of raw and other materials, capital, markets and others.

The framework of equal economic conditions legislatively created for enterprises irrespective of their forms of ownership opens up the possibilities for an unbiased assessment of the advantageous forms of production organization. Competition between enterprises with various forms of ownership encourages the improvement of the internal system of production management, technical retooling, the impovement of the responsiveness to new achievements in science and technology, of manufacturing the better quality goods at low costs and cheaper prices. In the long run this proves to be a powerful lever of economic, scientific and technological progress.

In the course of privatization there appears a chance not only to change the forms of ownership to eliminate sectoral monopolistic structures with narrow specialization formed in the conditions of the so-called single national economic complex. It should be born in mind that if privatization keeps the monopolistic position of some productions and enterprises playing the key role in the Republican market, it could be rather more dangerous for the economy of the Republic than when they are kept being state-owned.

Being out of the direct state control, monopolized non-state enterprises in the transition period will try to cover all production costs and to offer high wages through the monopolistic boosting of prices that becomes one of the reasons for the high level of inflation. Therefore, while implementing the measures on privatization of the monopolized structures, it is necessary, if allowed by the technological cycle, to ensure the conversion of the production itself into small scale enterprises, i.e. to demonopolize it. As a rule, the more mobile and compact productions can easily and better adapt to the market requirements. The investments applied to their reconstruction will bring return in the shorter period.

It is necessary to crucially reduce the number of enterprises subject to privatization constraints; anti-monopoly regulation measures need to be tightened through imposing progressive tax rates on the beyond-monopoly profit.

Diversification of the production structure is the most important aspect of privatization in terms of ensuring competitiveness for the nationalized enterprises. At present we have abolished the constraints that bound the privatized enterprises to maintain former profits for a certain period of time. It opens up new possibilities which allow, alongside with the change of the form of ownership, to crucially change the structure of the products, to start manufacturing marketable products which would be competitive both in the internal and external markets.

To ensure stability of enterprises in the post-privatization period, it is necessary to extensively use the procedure of changing the structure of production, providing the estimation of the financial potentials of enterprises as well as the development of projects for their technical, technological, organizational and economic transformation with regard to the market requirements.

The formation of the competitive environment and further development of market relations should also be promoted through the active support for the development of the emerging non-state structures. Privatization is not the only way to form the non-state sector of economy. There is the second powerful stream — that is initiating small- and medium-size enterprises based either on the individual private ownership or in the form of various limited liability companies; cooperatives, associations, societies. In countries with the developed market relations such kind of enterprises comprises about a half of their total number.

This is a very important source giving each person an opportunity to try himself in establishing his own business, to display his talent and to reveal his potentials. Thanks to this source it becomes possible to create a great number of jobs and to solve the problem of employment of both urban and rural population without large investments. Through the development of small enterprises equipped with the compact technological equipment it becomes possible to promote in short time the production of competitive goods, to saturate the domestic market with them and to fill in the gaps in the whole production cycle which cannot be filled by the large scale, specialized productions.

Therefore the state is obliged to render every kind of assistance to the development of small productions, to simplify the procedure of their establishment and registration, to create favourable taxation treatment for them, to provide them with the wide access to the credit and material resources ensure the freedom of business and external economic activities. The small non-state enterprises should be reliably protected by the law and by the whole authority of the state executive power. We need to develop and implement mainly during the second stage the integrated programme of the development in all spheres of the small business economy and to provide government support to it.

We should treat small business, private entrepreneurship as the factor promoting the accelerated economic development of our Republic.

It is the private sector that is the most mobile and the most initiative one. It is the private sector that, if given favourable conditions for the development, is able to help our economy to get out of the crisis. When the main part of the production comes from the private, non-state sector, then we may say with confidence that the economy has become really free and has acquired its future.

Naturally, in some spheres of economy the state owner enterprises should be maintained. The experience of France, Japan, Italy and other states with developed market economies testify that even within the market conditions the state sector continues to play the important role. There are practically no countries where the role of the state sector has been reduced to zero.

Consequently, while devising privatization programmes on the one hand, we need to precisely outline the limited group of enterprises should not become subject of privatization. On the other hand, it is necessary to work out the mechanism of management for these enterprises to enable them to adapt to the market conditions. The state enterprises should have maximum economic freedom and their activities should be commercialized. Maintaining the state form of ownership, these enterprises should not have much difference from the non-state enterprises in regard to the mechanism of management, conditions of profit distribution and material incentives. On the contrary, it is quite possible that in certain areas of activities especially those relating to the creation of the production structures being new to the country, they should be offered some special privileges. This in no way contradicts the market transformations deal that is underway in the country; moreover, it is aimed at strengthening economic and national independence of the country.

Proceeding from the elaborately fundamental propositions laid in the basis of the privatization process and taking into consideration the already accumulated experience, we set up main goals of further consolidation of the process of denationalization and privatization in the Republic as following:

— to expand the scale of privatization through the involvement of medium and large enterprises of priority sectors and spheres of economy into this process;

— to convert the monopolistic production and management structures into small ones and to create the competitive market environment;

— to improve privatization facility providing for the participation of various strata of society and foreign legal and natural entities in this conversion;

— to render every kind of assistance to the converted enterprises during post-privatization period;

— to create full-fledged market of securities and real estate.

According to these goals, the main avenues of the further development and deepening of the privatization process should be as follows.

First, henceforth, the conversion of state enterprises into other forms of ownership should be carried out on the basis of the specially designed sectoral and regional privatization programmes.

There have been created and are being implemented in the Republic the programmes that will have provided for the privatization about two thousand objects by the year of 1995. Half of these objects will be privatized through sectoral programmes and the rest — through local programmes. The programmes will cover industry, capital construction, transport and communications as well as social and other spheres.

During the second stage, the process of denationalization and privatization will be implemented in the key branches of industry: fuel and energy, mining, machine building and cotton processing complexes. Thus, in 1995 it is planned to convert into smaller ones 11 objects of the "Uzbekneftegas" corporation system, 17 objects under the Ministry of Energy, 22 objects under "Uzmashprom" association. Extended front privatization will be implemented in other sectors of the economy as well.

The process of conversion and privatization will go on in the sphere of transport, including bus and taxi depots, envisioning selling transportation vehicles to be owned privately.

Great attention will be attached to the privatization of tourist complexes in the cities of Bukhara, Samarkand, Khiva and Tashkent through tender sale, converting them into joint-stock companies, setting up joint ventures with foreign partners.

Second, the centre of privatization process will be shifted from the sectoral, Republican level to the territorial level. It is necessary to raise the status, broaden the rights and enhance the responsibility of the territorial bodies for the implementation of the conversion and privatization processes.

Third, the process of conversion of large and medium enterprises into open-end joint-stock companies, should become the main way of privatization. In so doing the already established closed and joint-stock companies should be converted into open companies.

The wide strata of population as well as foreign natural and legal entities should obtain wide access to the process of conversion of enterprises into joint-stock companies. All those willing to invest a part of their funds into the shares of large enterprises should be provided with such an opportunity. For this it is necessary to hold open auctions of securities, to expand the activities of the stock exchange, to create the infrastructure of the securities market through establishing investment companies, investment funds, clearing and agents' networks. The process of conversion of any enterprise into a joint-stock company should be open and public. It is necessary to widely explain to the population the terms of distribution of shares and the process of dividends pay-out.

Forth, the whole success of privatization far and foremost depends on privatization in rural areas. Today one of the important tasks is to create conditions for the appropriate organization of private farms and their sustainable functioning. To achieve this, it is necessary to devise the state investment programmes for the development of private farming, providing participation of foreign investors in the agricultural production and allot plots of land to the farmers for life possession.

It is necessary to expand selling plots of land under the trade and public services objects which are being privatized or have been already privatized, to sell plots of land to build offices, small enterprises, shops and public services objects. The auctions and tenders on transfer of agricultural lands into permanent use with succession must be conducted more frequently.

In the past we failed to start the mass sale of the plots of land. The experience of the developed countries testifies that there is no market economy without land market. Who will build a capital house, a shop, a small enterprise on the land which does not belong to him? Without providing people with lands we will fail to inspire in them the confidence in the future, the confidence that their children and grandchildren would be able to use the yield of their labour.

At the second stage the special attention should be paid to the further improvement of privatization mechanisms. It is necessary to elaborate and implement the mechanism of mass privatization which would provide wider involvement of population in privatization, to open for them the wide access to the securities market. More than 50 per cent of equities of the enterprise under privatization, must be subject to free sale.

There should be developed such a mechanism of privatization that would promote inviting direct foreign investments and technologies. It is necessary to expand and to improve practices of tenders and auctions, special investments auctions, all sorts of competitions. At the second stage tenders and auctions should become the primary means of denationalization and privatization.

The activities of the stock-exchange and real-estate exchange require to be further developed. Accelerated rates of denationalization, setting up open joint-stock companies, open up qualitatively for them. Simultaneously with followed-up shaping of primary markets of securities and real estate, the special emphasis should be shifted to the creation and development of the secondary markets. These are the secondary markets that must promote the sharp decrease of the portion of shares owned by the state, liquidation of loss-making and bankrupt enterprises, natural flow and turnover of securities, increase of their liquidity.

At the second state the special attention should be paid to the creation of the conditions necessary for the efficient functioning of the privatized enterprises, for the active back-up to entrepreneurship. Receipts obtained from denationalization and privatization should be primarily used for the support of the enterprises in the post-privatization period. Besides, it is expedient to allot these receipts for the realization of the most efficient investment projects, for the development of science intensive productions and changing profit of the privatized entreprises so that they could manufacture products following the market developments.

The realization of the mapped out measures armed at deepening process of privatization and creation of the competitive environment will allow to make another step along shaping up market economy.

2.2. ACHIEVING MACRO-ECONOMIC STABILIZATION IS THE PRIORITY OF THE ECONOMIC REFORM'S STRATEGY

At the new stage of the economic reform the economic and financial stability acquires the prior importance as a main precondition for structural transformations, recovery of the economy, its further dynamic and balanced development. The stabilization of economy is a natural and inevitable process on the part of shaping up market, aimed at overcoming the crisis. The effectiveness of the stabilization measures first and foremost depends on what we mean by the economic crisis and stabilization, on how we interpret them and what criteria is used to evaluate them.

Over many decades we have been brought up and tought such dogma that envisioned no economic crisis in the socialist system, that crisis was considered to be the major sin of the capitalist system. These dogma also envisioned situations under socialism when production relations lag behind from rapid development of productive forces and the results in certain discrepancies. And for this purpose there was the wise Gosplan (State Planning Committee), and above it the Central Committee that resolutely, in administrative way could restore the balance between the level of productive forces and the character of production relatons through the system plans and guidelines.

Nevertheless, these phenomena determined the fallaciousness of the system where the correspondence between the level of productive forces and production relations was achieved not through the economic laws but through the artificial decisions, through additional material inputs, through additional capital injections for the creation of the illusion of proportion purposes.

In the long run, the intensification of production by any got locked in itself, encouraged manufacturing unneeded products that could hardly find the market. The state artificially created the illusion of social usefulness of any goods produced in the conditions of the social system, thus giving rise to the economic irresponsibility of the producers themselves and leading to high production costs. The economy was becoming self-absorbing. Eventually, the shortage of material resources and raw materials became the most burning problem; their extensive utilization resulted in their depletion and inadequate application of natural wealth.

Nevertheless, in such a situation, precrisis expectations become that powerful, precautionary signal, pushing lever that in its turn in order to escape the complete failure, forces to undertake preventive measures for changing the structure of production and output, to strive for the reduction of production cost, to improve consumer qualities of goods, increase their competitiveness. The quest for escaping deep production crisis, puts enterprises up to look for and implement updated achievements of science and advanced technology. In the long run, all these efforts are aimed at stable production in the conditions of tough competitiveness, preventing break-up which that read to the balance between the market demand and supply on a global scale.

That, vice of the capitalist overproduction that we were tough to consider its main drawback, actually turned out to be a powerful impetus for the economic development and improvement of economic relations.

While devising the adjustment programme it is **important to concentrate on not only overcoming the crisis itself, not on the improving indicators which are just the barometer of state of an economy, but rather profoundly examine the inner causes which led the country to the crisis,** to respond in due time to the deviations and discrepancies arising, to actively undertake measures to preventing the crisis.

The adjustment policy first of all is the targeted state policy for maintaining the macro-economic equilibrium, avoidance of crucial recession and mass unemployment, for ensuring inflation level and emission management, for the balance of payment maintenance.

The goal of the stabilization is to avoid and, if necessary, to improve domestic and foreign imbalance which can eventually result in an unmanagable economic recession.

The world practice has produced several significantly different approaches to the implementation of the stabilization policies; following are the most typical of them:

first, monetarist approach is being based on the suppression of the inflation level, stabilization of currency circulation by means of abrupt reduction of money stock and aggregate capacity to pay. This approach does not ensure deep economic transformations, on the contrary, it often leads to the reduction of output, freezing up of investment activities;

second approach is being based on the stimulation of the production and enterpreneurship activities, on the promotion the structural transformations and elimination of discrepancies in economy along with the measures based on the moderately tight fiscal and monetary policies, constraining excessive demand that is not backed up that goods.

Our approach is as follows: we can overcome the deep protracted crisis, we have found ourselves in without social upheavals and exploions through reliance on production, on those who create material values. We are supported by those who produce goods, cultivate land, erect buildings, constructions and new production capacities.

Recently, it has become fashionable, especially in the CIS countries, to believe that we have reached the line, the watershed, the moment of choice — either to favour the monetarist approaches where tight anti-inflationary measures dominate in the macroeconomic policy, establish their rule, dictate their requirements which would enable us to reduce the inflation rate down to 1-2% which is the major outcome of adjustment, or the economy and the society reach the verge of complete collapse, full degradation.

Instead of realizing again what "shock therapy" represents, instead of being convinced that without strong social policies, the reform will be discredited and doomed to fail and will lead to the social outburst, there is coming another wave; they say that due to certain political considerations for a long time we have been very cautions about certain issues relating to liberalization and found ourselves at the final verge. It seems that the time has come to realize, to think over the two- or three-year experience of the reforms which showed that the one-sided monetarist approach is unacceptable for the countries of the former Soviet Union with their deformed, highly monopolized and narrow specialization economy, low living standards of the bulk of the population.

Whole talking about transition to market such apologists of the new economic policy have driven their countries into recession, into exchange in kind (even the "in kind" wages have become the mass phenomenon), have carried the market exchange to the point of absurdity, and now they are advocating this method as the one that can put down the inflation, create the civilized system, ensure the recovery of production.

However, there is a direct contradiction — there can be no recovery of production under such so-called macro-economic policies. It is the height of absurdity. Production cannot be opposed to inflation.

Not abrupt, but gradual decrease of production is allowed only to those limits which seem inevitable to ensure its structural modifications. In other words, for achieving its progressive structure in the most simple words — for the production of those, which can hold cold water and can ensure meeting consumer requirements of the buyers.

Such drop in production can be explained as one of the manifestations of the period of transition from one centralized command and planning system to another — to the free market economy.

As soon as the market laws start working, the real competitive environment becomes established and the ways for free entrepreneurship are opened up there will appear the structural diversification of production under these laws. It will happen to those who want to stand the competition. There will be created conditions that would encourage the constant renewal of production to make it able to stand the competition.

During the transition period, while divising and implementing the economic policies the state should bear in mind that it must promote in every way possible the development of the priority, promising sectors and productions, i.e. to find out the most important key links (oil — oil independence; energy — energy independence; grain — bread independence; cotton processing industry, etc.) and thus to carry out the consistent policy of structural transformation of the economy.

We should invest into these priority sectors to ensure their structural character, not only their development but their internal structural transformations as well. Otherwise the economy will came to chaos. **Without determining priority key sectors, without supporting their is shaping up in the conditions of market relations we will not only lose economic strategy but also fail to ensure the logical consistency of the transformations which are supposed to bring the production up to the qualitatively new level.** As soon as the real market conditions are created they themselves will promote and direct the production and eventually will result in the growth of production.

Consequently, the monetarism has never been the only driving and determining force which would be able to ensure the overcoming of the crisis. **While developing the adjustment programme it is necessary to rely upon not tight monetarism as** such but rather to maintain a well balanced monetary policy along with the policy of support for the key sectors and structural transformations. The priority number one is to determine strategic guide-line proceeding from the found out priorities is to apply macro-economic policies for it.

This is not our intention to sacrifice development priorities for the sake of the macro-economic balance. Alongside with the reforms we strive to ensure the state and economic independence.

Proceeding from these provisions we set the following main criteria to achieve the economic stabilization:

— not to allow the decrease of the volume of output if it is not connected with structural transformations and technical retooling of production;

— to create favourable conditions for the output increase in the priority sectors, to promote encouraging production activities. We cannot hope for financial and social stability without support of our own production and growth of economy from inside through the utilization of the domestic resources;

— to ensure within the reasonable limits the stability of state budget and financial position of the enterprises;

— to suppress inflation processes. Only efficient antiinflationary measures can help to achieve strengthening of the national currency, activization of domestic long-term investment market, maintenance of the stable living standards of the population;

— to use all the means to improve the balance of payments and state hard currency reserves and on this basis to strengthen the stand of Uzbekistan in terms of relations as well as maintaining stable exchange rate of "soum" against the hard currencies;

— to ensure the balance of the strong social policy for stabilization of social conditions strengthening and to maintain the living standards of population, as far as possible.

In this respect, at the second stage of the reform the following should become one of the most important and primary measures for stabilization of the economy: implementation of tight fiscal policy aimed at reduction of the state budget deficit within the minimum allowable limits (about 3-4 per cent of the gross domestic product). The observance of budget discipline is one of the determining stabilization factors. Increase of the budget deficit should always be considered as an alarm.

The most important goal of the budget policy during the second stage of the reform is to ensure the optimum correlation between the solution of the stabilization of the economy tasks at the expense of reducing budget deficit and financing the current socially significant costs which encourage the revival of the economic activities. **The efforts to balance the budget only through the further sharp reduction of the state expenditures which are necessary for the current consumption and restructuring of the economy may result in the deterioration of the economic situation and dragging out of the reforming process.**

During this stage the major objective is to halt the recession of the production along with the implementation of necessary structural transformations. State expenditures, their breakdown should be arranged in such a way so that could be aimed at achieving of above objectives and in so doing could promote transition to market processes in all possible way.

Improvement of the taxation has the significant role to play in the solution of problems relating to the stabilization of the economy and strengthening of the financial position. In the conditions of transition to the market relations the taxes become the main regulator of the economic policy implementation. As an integral part of the very process of transformations and its internal booster, the taxation system should to the largest extent correspond to the purposes of the economic transformation. First of all, the taxation system should completely fulfill its direct functions, i.e.— fiscal, redistribution and encouraging ones.

Being the key element of the fiscal policy the taxes are called upon to ensure the revenue part of the state budget in the amounts necessary for the solution of the most important general state and national economy plans.

Being combined with the targeted fiscal policy, the taxation system redistributes the part of gross domestic product and therefore participates in the structural transformation of the economy, in ensuring social guarantees for the population.

The most important function of the taxation system is its stimulating influence on the development of production, efficient utilization of material resources and raw materials, natural, financial and man power resources, property accumulation.

At the second stage of the reform when the economic stabilization and structural transformation become **the immediate** tasks, the taxation system should **mainly ful**fil its stimulating function. This required the profound transformation of the whole existing system of taxation.

The main principle assumed as a basis for transformation of the taxation system is the sharp reduction of the taxation burden being imposed upon enterprises. The high enterprise income tax rate gave no possibility for an enterprise to allocate funds for the development of production, technical retooling, replenishment of their working capital and this in the long run resulted in the recession in production. Moreover, maintaining heavy tax burden for a long time threatens with danger to indirectly maintain the high inflation rate. This is endangered by the fact that in the conditions of recession, the increase of tax revenues can happen only as a result of the inflation growth of profits of an enterprise. This is very close to the collapse of the financial system, to the stagnant production, aggravation of social problems.

Shift from the taxation of incomes on the taxation of profits along with the decrease of taxation burden, opens up the possibility for the intensive production and business activities. The increase of the profit stock which remains at the disposal of the enterprises will not only strengthen their financial position but will lead to the revival of their investment activities which would serve as a basis for the structural transformations, both productional and technological ones.

The wider economic freedom for enterprises must result in not only the increase of the total profit stock assigned for the extended reproduction but at the same time will open up the possibility to increase the wages of the workers. For the time being the economic environment is being created to stimulate business activities, give each person an opportunity to realize his potentials and to make earnings relevant to his or her involvement in these activities. Under such conditions the taxes on the physical persons should, on the one hand, stimulate the workers to actively participate in the social production and, on the other hand, promote the adequacy between the wages and the labour inputs in order to avoid the ungrounded differentiation in terms of incomes by population.

In the long run reducing tax burden of enterprises, and decreasing VAT rate should result in resuscitation of the production which is of great importance for the challenges relating to the stabilization process in economy.

Within the frameworks of the new taxation policy there was set forth the task to crucially modify tax receipts structure, to increase the role of taxes on resources, to introduce the progressive taxation system to be levied on physical persons' incomes.

Regretably, until recently such types of taxes as land tax, tax on entrails and water tax have been neglected. Enterprises were permitted to wholesale exterminate the most valuable, unreplenishible natural resources, without accounting for the environmental protection, thereby robbing themselves and their posterity.

As long as natural resources deplete, we should be more careful, not to repeat past years mistakes. For this purpose we are supposed to extensively use economic levers, by means of taxes to insure everybody to utilize natural and raw materials with maximum efficiency.

There exists another side of this problem. Taxes do constrain utilization of raw materials, thereby we encourage reduction of the production cost, self-cost of the products, stimulate appliance of the updated ecologically pure technologies and what is the most important, non-waste technologies. Therefore, increasing payments for resources pursue several aims simultaneously, i.e. encourage scientific, technical and social progress in the most broad sense.

Differentiation between the Republican and local taxes as sources of budget receipts is the most important avenue for improvng taxation. **It would be essential to allocate the major part of the state budget receipts to the local budgets in order to strengthen them.** It would enable regions to strive for being more independent, more resourceful and responsible in terms of the budget execution. Besides, this would encourage them to look for new sources of receipts to the local budgets and would strengthen the budget discipline on the spot.

Therefore, taxation reform is called upon creating incentives for economic stabilization, intensification of the production and labour motivities, serving strong facility for implementation of the priorities and challenges of the second stage of the reform process.

Strengthening finance discipline of the enterprises, stabilization of the settlement system, solution of the arrear problems are very important in line of budget balance and improvement of fiscal policies as well.

Today many people believe that drop in the production is the result of the collapse of trade relations among former republics, the result of the arrears among the CIS enterprises, customs borders. This is a primitive and simplified approach which is far from true. Emerged borders had their negative role to play in terms of establishing high tariffs for transport and higher customs duties.

It is a misconception that emerged borders are the reason for arrears. Curtailing raw material supplies, components and products to a less extent were resulted from the collapse of trade economic and cooperation relations. **If to proceed from the conception that emerging borders are the result of the trade collapse, what will be the explanation then for existing arrears and problems with supplies in Russia itself where the amount of arrears is huge.**

What is the true reason for this? The point is that under the old system supplies of products from one enterprise to the other one irrespective of the location were centralized and the allocated funds existed for this purpose. And then it was subject to the State Supplies Committee to decide what specific enterprises in the Far East should supply their products to what specific consumers in Moscow and vice versa. The same was true of redistribution of products among the republics. **In other words products were distributed among suppliers and consumers all over the Union no matter whether or not they were needed, marketable or met international requirements. And the consumer, that was indicated in the distribution schedule was supposed to accept them and to supply their products to the other enterprises in its turn.**

Settlements for natural supplies were maintained by the centralized system itself. In accordance with the established requirements, banks debited accounts of the enterprises and carried out settlements for the above supplies. By the end of the year, arrears as a rule were settled through the **so-called inter-departmental offsets which were maintained in a centralized way as well.** Credits to repay arrears were extended in a centralized way as well as applied for mutual discharge.

All over again started from the next year, went over the new cycle. **Such system did not envision such notions as competition, balance of demand and supply on a market basis** and what is the most important, there were no conditions created for an enterprise to be able to manufacture needed and competitive products.

The foreign trade relations of the so-called single national economy complex of the Union were maintained at the expense of the centralized foreign exchange fund in the first turn and at the expense of the receipts from oil, gas, timber, gold, mineral resources, cotton and armament sales.

All this was managed by the center **and eventually resulted in the overcentralized system which decided everything what to produce and in what quantities within the closed Union system without counting on the actual demand.**

All this should have been finished sooner or later due to the limited raw material resources and it would be impossible to keep up production with a reliance on the domestic resources in the closed system. It resulted in not only stagnant economic life but in recession of the technical progress and reluctance to accept the scientific and technological achievements, in lagging behind the world economic developments.

That system scheduled everything — what region supplies raw materials, what regions process them and destinations to supply them. In this system Uzbekistan had to play the role of the main supplier of cotton, gas, gold, non-ferrous and terra rara metals, fruit and vegetables. In so doing all this was supplied at the artificially low fixed prices excluding labour input and world price developments for such raw materials.

In other words, the role of Uzbekistan in this closed system was strictly predetermined and we could not leave this closed circle. Just one example, we couldn't ensure deep processing and manufacturing of the finished products made of caprolactame which we extracted from the Uzbek gas or processing and manufacturing nitron products at the Chirchik and Navoi chemical plants with their polluting and explosive productions, just because similar plants were already built in Byelorussia, Russia and Ukraine and according to the all-union division of labour we were supposed to supply them with raw materials. I can draw many examples like this one.

We must bear in mind the fact that processes relating to obtaining independence by the former USSR countries are connected with the general shelving the unjustified administrative and command centalized system product redistribution and shifting to the free market economy. **Today we are in the process of creation of the properly new economy to be relying upon market laws, when products are manufactured depending on demand need and supply viewing it should be competitive and meet international requirements.** No enterprise entering the market track can build its future without considering markets and competition inherent in the market being environment. An enterprise will have prospects when it maintains mutual cooperation relations and can market its products at least to those who supplies it with the components.

It should become a requirement that a considerable portion of their products must be sold in other regions for the foreign exchange in first turn. And this foreign exchange on the enterprises' accounts will serve the finance base to cover all expenditures relating to purchasing machinery, components and technological updating. Only such a base can become a reliable foundation to ensure reasonable, mutually beneficial cooperation, improving, well-being of both the enterprise and the employees.

The heads of the enterprises should get it clear once and for all that only foreign exchange receipts available on enterprises' accounts will enable them to provide supplies of any components and materials from any region, from any part of the world. Only such prospects can get us out of crisis and ensure the growth of production. Then there will be no need for enterprises — associations to wheedle exchange raw materials, i.e. raw cotton and cotton products, non-ferrous metals and others to be bartered in the humiliating transactions. **Then there will be no need to appeal to the so-called collapse of economic relations, arrear problems and "parade of soreveignities."**

We are aware of the fact that in any case it would be essential to remove the artificial barriers and borders so that goods, capital, man power could cross them freely and to reduce crippling customs duties and high transportation tariffs. But nevertheless one should not be under misapprehension that all these impediments are the major reasons for the drop of production, discontinued enterprises and arrear problems.

The major reason lies in the necessity of conducting structural changes in the production and termination of those productions that manufacture irrelevant goods.

At the contemporary phase of the economic reformation process strengthening of the banking and credit systems, money circulation, regulation of the foreign market is gaining in the major importance.

The adjustment programmes should be aimed at significant reduction of the external lending. Bank credits should be advanced in first turn to those who can increase the output of the strategically important products, consumer goods and to ensure their timely repayment. But at the same time we should have firm hold in terms of preventing unjustified credit emission and outflow of loan funds.

Everyone should understand one truth — extending credits to those who is unable to increase the output of the consumer goods and other needed products, would increase the inflationary process and undermine stability of the national currency. This is the reason why every soum being put into circulation must be backed up by goods.

The major objective of the monetary policies reform is the creation of the appropriate conditions to overcome crisis and recover the national economy through gradual reduction of inflation and creation of prerequisites to provide the production stability.

It is essential to establish strict control over the inflation level and to ensure efficients anti-inflationary measures. Considerable reduction of the inflation rates is the pivot of the adjustment policies at the contemporary stage.

As this takes place we must take a realistic approach in terms of making choice of the desired inflation rates. Achieving artificially low inflation rates and applicance of all possible means and ways for it, is not always justified, especially when it results in the economic recession. **Artificial suppression of the inflation without considering its original reason is threatening with its recurrence and might cause aggravation of the crisis rather than its overcoming.**

It is important to note that establishing control over inflation taken apart, is not the proof of the successful implementation of the adjustment programme. Inflation is an indicator of deep discrepancies in the economy needed to be reconciled.

Economic disproportions normally lie in the basis of any inflation. Therefore combatting inflation presupposes not only suppresing it, but rather conducting tight structural policies to be aimed at eliminating discrepancies that are taking place in the economy. The experience of some foreign countries in curbing inflation shows that realizing unsolvable relations between inflation and structural economic deformations, they did not bind themselves on the tight management of circulation sphere alone and eliminating excessive aggregate capacity to pay but rather have developed and implemented large-scale investment targeted programmes that enabled them to eliminate the above discrepancies and, consequently, reasons causing the inflation.

Macro-economic adjustment is not an end in itself to us. It is important rather as vitally necessary stage of the creation of the relevant conditions and prerequisites for resuscitation of the economy and its structural transformations, enhancing investment activities, increasing the number of jobs, output of the competitive goods and the growth of real incomes of the population.

2.3. STRENGTHENING NATIONAL CURRENCY IS THE KEY OBJECTIVE OF THE NEW PHASE OF THE ECONOMIC REFORM

In the strategy of the economic reform underway in our young state, special significance is attached to the solution of the problems relating to the introduction and stable circulation of the own national currency. **National currency is the pride of the nation, the symbol of the state independence, the attribute of the sovereign state. This is the common wealth and property of the Republic.**

Introduction effective from July 1, 1994 of the full-fledged national currency — soum as the only legal tender on the territory of Uzbekistan, was a revolutionary step indeed, and has marked the beginning of the qualitatively new phase of the reform process in the economy. We have obtained the real mechanism for the implementation of our own, independent of somebody's will, finance, monetary and economic policies to meet the interests of the people of Uzbekistan. For this event we have been making long and thorough preparations. The experience of the first months of new currency circulation showed that it has become the powerful factor for the economic adjustment, strengthening financial position of the enterprises and sectors of the economy, factor for the social protection of the population and the consumer market of the country.

For today our priority is to make our currency strong, and respectable in the world. It should have its dignity and strength. Ensuring stability and high authority of "soum" is the national challenge, the solution of which will have impact on well-being and prosperity of all citizens of our country. Therefore, the strategic priority of the second phase of the reform processes is the further strengthening of the soum.

We need to achieve its domestic current account convertibility so that it could be freely exchanged for hard currencies. The well-being of each of us, of every resident of the country, all enterprises depends on the stability of circulation of the national currency.

Stability of the national currency, its domestic convertibility must be backed up by the sufficient amount of competitive products, by necessary reserves. For this purpose we have developed and are still implementing four targeted integrated programmes aimed at the solution of the specific problems.

First, own national currency is actually strong and authoritative only when it has the reliable commodity coverage. In order to increase the purchasing power of the soum it would be required to saturate the Republican market with the consumer goods both imported and produced domestically.

The major objective is to increase the domestic output of the goods that would meet the most vital needs of the people. For this purpose we will provide all possible assistance to the enterprises manufacturing goods for people irrespective of their form of ownership, and these enterprises will be of our priority in terms having access to investments, raw materials and credit resources.

One can actually feel these positive developments in this respect. The output of the consumer goods is being increased year after year. The share of the own produce in the gross sales volume of the consumer goods is growing. But at the same time we are much dependent on the import of the whole range of essential foodstuffs such as grain, sugar, powder milk, food alcohol as well as some sorts of non-food goods, for every day living especially. We have to put up with this as soon as possible.

For these purposes it would be necessary to reorient all our industries to manufacturing quality consumer goods meeting exacting tastes of our buyers. It would be essential to be bolder in arranging new productions for manufacturing updated consumer goods, to create space for activities of small enterprises which are able to promptly response to changing demand of the population, and market developments.

Our people who have undergone terrible ordeals, who at this complicated transition time are full of willingness to change their life for the better and do their best for it, are entitled to have nutritious food, nice clothes and have decent living conditions. And our duty is to create such conditions for them.

It is essential to alley the psychology of both our manufacturers and consumers. We should be proud of the fact that we produce, buy and wear goods of our own production. It offends the national dignity when manufactured goods find no buyer, when their quality leaves much to be desired. This is the proof of not only neglecting their responsibilities, which is not true of our hard working people. This is the highway robbery of themselves, of their country, of their people. We should achieve "made in Uzbekistan" products be welcome in any part of the world and require no additional advertising.

By known reasons until recently we had no possibility to have our market saturated with all necessary domestically produced goods. And even today the share of the imported goods in the commodity turnover breakdown is very high and imported goods are very popular with the population. Henceforth, we should create all necessary conditions for our population to buy qualitative goods from different countries of the world. In every way we will encourage importers of vitally important tradable food stuffs and manufactured goods. Today there have been abolished all import duties. But all together we will improve the import structure by having protected our consumers' interests from poor quality and hazardous for health goods and costly produce.

By stimulating imports at the same time we have set the objectives through increasing competitiveness of our products to upbring our population in the spirit of buying domestically produced goods. One cannot be a true patriot if worshipping all the imported.

Second, stable functioning of the currency, its stability, convertibility depend on the availability of sufficient foreign exchange reserves. Only then our currency will be recognized and respected when it can be freely converted into any hard currency. For this purpose it would be necessary to radically revise all our foreign trade policies.

We have repeatedly emphasized that one of the priorities of the reformation process is the expansion of the export potential, changing profile of enterprises in favour of manufacturing products for export, conquering strong holds in the world market. More than once we have been noting that only those enterprises who have made their choice in favour of building up output for export, would have privileges in terms of supplies with raw materials and investments. This is our guideline.

We must create such incentives, such levers which would enable enterprises to fully turn to the manufacturing goods competitive in the world market. As soon as possible they must enter the world markets with the products which could stand any cold water, to learn making hard currency, to replenish the Republican Treasury. This is their must, their holy duty before their state, their colleagues, the whole people.

Third, the national currency will become the real legal tender when any enterprise, any individual learns to value every earned soum. We must learn to respect national currency, to be proud of it, to take care of it. Currency is the measure and appreciation of labour of every citizen.

For this purpose tight monetary policies should be pursued. We will have to be zealous, prudent and cautions in utilizing our funds, not to allow to get them scattered. Every soum spent and invested in the national economy should bring solid return, it should work for tomorrow, for the prospects of the country.

Enterprises, entrepreneurs should be aware of the fact that the state funds, state credits being advanced to them are not just grants. Unconditional responsibility for effective and targeted utilization of the funds obtained should become an indisputable law. Credit recovery should be very high. Therefore, terms of credits should be such that enterprises could feel their responsibility for credits obtained and could utilize them for increasing their output with maximum efficiency.

Forth, the most important condition for the strengthening of the national currency is maintaining strong, well-weighted anti-inflationary policies. Sharp reduction of the inflation rate — that is what can make national currency stable. This is the guarantee for strength and health of our young currency.

The national currency "Soum" will become mighty and authoritative when it remains solvent for a long time. Each of us could already feel that our soum has been endoured with such strength. The level of infation has significantly dropped. And these positive tendencies should be enhanced. There should become the firm rule: every soum being put in circulation must be embodied in goods, invisible and it should work for the prosperity of a family. It is essential to radically improve the work of trading enterprises. Today all of them have been privatized. It is important to arrange their work in such a way that trading enterprises could compete among themselves for a buyer, could work for him, for meeting his demands.

We must not, and have no right to allow the money stock that is not backed by the relevant growth of goods and services to grow.

Unrestrained growth of money holdings with the population when there is scarcety of goods will ultimatly result in price increase in first turn, new spire of inflation. This is threatened with danger of emerging exclusive, vicious circle which might untwist runaway inflation.

Therefore, the scarcety of goods and services in the domestic consumer market under the conditions of their monopoly production and distribution, price liberalization, urges manufacturers and trading enterprises to boost up prices. It results in reduction of real wages, limiting purchasing power of the population and the level of its actual consumption. For the purpose of protection of the interests of the population, prevention of the abrupt deterioration of the living standards of the people, the state has to undertake measures on income indexation of the population, increasing minimum and average wages, pensions and scholarships. Payable demand is growing, but it cannot be met without increasing output of consumer goods and services. The shortage of goods and price increase are over there again, there is a new round but of the other, more catastrophic scales. So it will continiously go on if no specific resolute measures are undertaken to curb this baneful spiral. Ascending, spiral-like growth of money stock and prices will inevitably cause prolonged inflation and it, in its turn will result in losing control over economy, degradation of the whole production, destitution of the population and social upheavals, i.e. to the collapse of the whole economic system, restoration of which would require many years and huge funds.

Therefore, at the contemporary stage under insufficient saturation of the domestic market there would be required to restrain the growth of the consumption fund by putting it into direct dependence on increasing physical volumes of the output of goods and services. It is important to understand the simple truth — viewing acceleration if saturation of the domestic market with goods and services, today's stage of the reform must ensure by all means prevention of filling up the money issue with empty money.

Saturation of the •domestic market with goods is the most important condition for stability of the national currency and improvement of the living standard of the population. Owing to this it would be necessary to ensure control over the growth of the consumption fund and the growth of the output. Non-observance of this might result in a runaway inflation development.

Preventing growth of cash and credit issue, hoarding money by population is proving to be our priority. It is necessary to do the utmost to make funds advanced return, not to advance credits if production does not provide the growth of the output.

Implementation of the four mapped out programmes should facilitate strengthening of our national currency, stabilization of its exchange rate against other hard currencies.

In the open economy conditions which is true of Uzbekistan, stabilization of the exchange rate of the national currency is the important avenue of the macro-economic stabilization policies. Stable currency — stable import prices, and this will have positive impact on the overall price developments in the domestic market, will serve the mighty factor to down the inflation.

Effective from October 15, 1994 for the purpose of the real determination of the exchange rate irrespective of the currencies of other states we have launched the regular foreign exchange auctions at the Uzbek Republican Interbank Foreign Currency Exchange. The unified exchange rate that fluctuates depending on the demand and that supply for all sorts of foreign exchange transactions.

It is important to remark that at the initial stage of maintaining the foreign exchange transactions the priority was given to the increase of the foreign exchange transfers at the Interbank Foreign Currency Exchange.

Centralized export revenues, currency requirements as well as available foreign exchange of the enterprises are being regularly put on the foreign exchange auction to cover the demand for hard currency. In the course of 1994, since the start of the work of the Foreign Currency Exchange the volume of sales has increased by 5 times.

For the time being our objective is to bring the turnover of the Interbank Foreign Currency Exchange up to such a level that would allow any enterprise, entrepreneur or individual to exchange their money for hard currency or vice versa at any time and in any amount. For this purpose along with the measures undertaken on the expansion of export there have been signed the agreements with the International Monetary Fund and the World Bank on Extending the Institutional and Rehabilitation Loans to Uzbekistan. This would enable us to increase the total turnover of the Uzbek Republican Foreign Currency Exchange up to US $1.5 billion.

Effective from April 1995 there has been adopted the decision to hold the foreign exchange auctions not less than twice a week and further on even more frequently. The number of the participants in the hard currency exchange is subject to increase due to the pursued policies.

Successful implementation of the mapped out measures undoubtedly must bring the positive impact on stabilization of the exchange rate of the local currency, its strengthening and increasing its authority. I want to reiterate again incontestable truth — the economy is strong when the national currency is strong.

2.4. ACHIEVING DEEP-ROOTED STRUCTURAL TRANSFORMATIONS IS THE MAJOR CONDITION FOR THE SUSTAINABLE ECONOMIC GROWTH

The second stage of the economic reform will have to resolve the most important challenge which is of the strategic significance for the Republic — i.e. to lay the basis for deep-rooted structural transformations of our economy. Implementation of the radical structural modifications is one of the important conditions for achieving macro-economic stability and perspectively providing sustainable economic growth and well-being to the population of Uzbekistan, integration into the world economic system.

Everybody knows what state of the economy we have inherited — the overcentralized economy with distorted orientation to supplying mainly raw materials, with deep-rooted territorial disproportions, with outdated production assets. Therefore, in order to fling down the previous burden, to obtain true independence and economic freedom we would have to carry out structural transformations.

There has been set forth the objective to overcome the one-sided raw material orientation of our economy and to drastically alter its sectoral structure, to eliminate discrepancies in development and allocation of production forces as the result of the so-called "all-union specialization", to shift on manufacturing finished products, bring their quality and competitiveness up to the level of the world market requirements.

Structural policy is aimed at creation on the eve of the 21st century of the new, in its essence, national economy complex in Uzbekistan to guarantee the economic and political independence of the Republic and decent living conditions for its people.

For achieving this goal there would be required not only to reorganize the sectoral and territorial structure of our economy, export-import output structure, but first and foremost, it would be important to significantly reconcile the most essential macro-economic, reproductive proportions. In the long run we must achieve the optimal balance of the reproductive structure of the economy which would meet interests of both production and population.

Sectoral structure needs significant modifications. It is clear that it would be extremely complex to carry out the drastic changes over a short period of time and it would require huge investments. But already today we must do the utmost to turn our national economy to face the needs of the Republic and requirements of the population. The first steps in this direction have been already made. It is important to consolidate and follow them up.

Improvement of the territorial structure would require some special solution. Natural, resource and manpower potential of the Republic of Kazakhstan, regions are not used fully and efficiently enough. A lot of populated areas, villages with undeveloped production base, backward infrastructure are still present over there.

By the reorganization of the structure of the economy one should understand not only changes in the list of the manufactured products proceeding from the demand but rather relevant improvement of quality, reduction of the aggregate production cost as well. Consequently, changes in the production structure, overtaking development of the priority sectors should be without fail accompanied by liquidation of the loss-making enterprises and changing the profile of the enterprises manufacting incompetitive products. This aspect is not least important than creation of new enterprises.

When developing structural policies at the new phase of the structural reform we must rely upon those richest natural, mineral and manpower resources that are available and proceed from their most efficient utilization, from the priorities chosen, from determining the policy to be pursued.

Structural transformations in the economy are tied up to the solution of the following most important tasks.:

first, to obtain economic independence of the Republic at the expense of reduction of import of the most important raw materials, components and foodstuff through the development of import-substituting productions;

second, to ensure the needs of the population and the national economy as a whole to vitally essential types of products and consumer goods at the expense of arranging domestic production of these products;

third, to ensure the balanced and sustainable functioning of the economy;

fourth, to overcome the one-sided raw material orientation of the economy, to account deep procession of the richest mineral resources and agricultural raw materials, increasing the level of readiness and competitiveness of the products being manufactured;

fifth, to expand the export potential of the country, to achieve surplus in the foreign trade balance of payment, to strengthen gold and foreign exchange reserves;

sixth, to ensure the rational employment of manpower, to create new job-places to meet updated technologies' requirements, historic traditions and skills of the people;

and **seventh**, to eliminate intrasectoral and territorial disproportions, to accelerate the development and wise allocation of productive forces in the territory of the Republic.

For efficient transformation of our economy in compliance with the modern market requirements we must find out specific answers to the following questions:

— what avenues of the economy, what sectors and productions are our priorities for today, the development of which would require our efforts, funds and resources.

— what are the sourses of finance for manufacturing products to be tradable in the domestic and world market.

— how competitiveness of our products could be ensured.

The answers to these questions open up the way to social progress, wide implementation in the production of updated achievements of science and technique, advanced forms and methods of management, wide scale integration into the world economic system and occupy the deserved place within it.

In accordance with the determined objectives at the second phase of the reform the major avenues for structural changes in the economy will accelerate development of sectors, whole complexes ensuring the energy and foodstuff independence of the Republic, building up the potential of the interrelated sectors and productions which would ensure within shortest period of time the production of the finished competitive products on the basis of the available mineral resources and agricultural raw materials. Simultaneously, the traditional specialization of productions must provide the dynamic development when retooled with updated technologies and equipment.

At the second stage of the reform reproduction structure of the national economy must be drastically changed. Until we change the reproduction structure, until we pay serious attention to the reduction of production cost, until we achieve reduction in material consumption of the product, until we conduct resource-saving policies, we would never get rid of ominoius shortage of goods.

At the new stage it would be essential to ensure the optimal reconciliation between consumption and accumulation of funds, to create necessary conditions for resolving problems relating to the general economic stabilization and further growth of the economy. Optimization of the consumption fund has the important role to play in reconciliation between demand and supply in the domestic market, i.e. in ensuring the appropriate proportion between money stocks and their commodity back up. That's why the state should acquire the facility for otimal regulation over the most important macro-economic reproduction proportions.

At the second phase of the structural reforms the special priority will be given to the sectoral structural reforms and key sectors related to the accelerated development.

Considering that the Republic has to rely upon its own in its development, the life itself requires to develop the most important key sectors in first turn, i.e. oil and gas industry, energy, gold mining and other non-ferrous metals industries, communication networks and infrastructure.

Development of key sectors is the major condition for the economic independence of Uzbekistan. Given we ensure accelerated development of key sectors, find out all necessary investment sources it would create the reliable basis and favourable conditions for the dynamic development of the whole economy.

The Republic will be independent when it obtains energy independence. Until recently we had had to import mainly from the CIS countries vitally important oil, petroleum products and energy sources.

Today the situation has changed. Oil and gas outputs have been increased. Domestic output of the petroleum products has been increased as well, namely, the output of black oil, diesel oil, lubricants. New oil fields open up good prospects — Mingbulak and Kokdumalak oil fields need to be intensively developed. There should be intensified works relating to the construction of the Bukhara and remodelling of the Ferghana oil refineries. The tasks were out up complete construction of the Novoangren and the Talimarjan hydroelectric power stations and to increase the coal output as well.

Mining natural gas and other relatively cheap energy sources should have dominant place to occupy in the fuel balance of the country.

Along with this there would be necessary to conduct consistent energy saving policies, accelerate development of non-energy consuming productions that in their turn would enable to ensure progressive structural changes in the economy under the moderate development of the fuel and energy complex.

Structural policy in the metallurgical complex should be aimed at increasing the output of non-ferrous metals being the most important source of export revenues as well as those types of the products until present being imported from the CIS countries i.e. electrowelded tubes, brass, bronze and others. Overall remodelling of the Bekabad Metallurgical Plant running on the metal waste basis, the only enterprise in Central Asia which manufactures wide range of ferrous metals and hardware, is gaining in importance.

Development of the chemical industry should be based mainly on the more extensive development of domestic resources with the provision of environmentally clean productions. The whole chemical complex needs to be radically reorganized and reequipped.

Considering the Uzbekistan's resources of high content aromatic hydrocarbons available, as well as its mining potential, it would be essential to set up on this basis a large — scale complex to manufacture polyethylene, polypropelene, polystirol and other products which are in great demand in the domestic and world markets. In an effort to achieve the economic independence it is envisioned to set up production — capacities to process kaprolactame, kapron threads and staple fibre.

Dynamic development and increasing role of science intensive production is the most important priority of the sectoral structural policies. Orientation to the development of science intensive and technology consuming industries will resolve the strategic task i.e. strengthening Uzbekistan's hold in the world market, achieving economic and technological independence of the country.

Uzbekistan, unlike other Central Asian countries, is endowed with an extensive scientific and technical capability, strong experimental and production facilities. Our duty is to make them serve interests of the country and its people.

Development of agricultural machine building based on manufacturing cotton-pickers and components for the cotton processing complex of the country is still the most important avenue of the sectoral specialization. We cannot rely upon imports of cotton sowing, processing and harvesting machines due to the fact that such kind of machines have been manufactured by just two countries in the world, i.e. by the USA and Uzbekistan.

In the machine-building complex when downing production scales in the sectors which much depend on imports of raw materials and components there has been set forth an objective to expand the material base to provide manufacturing machines and components for deep procession of the local raw materials, technological equipment for the light and food industries, small mechanization divices for newly created farmers' (dekhkans') and personal subsidiary holdings, spare parts for the agricultural machinery and vehicles as well as production of the hi-tech home electronics and other consumer goods.

The future of Uzbekistan belongs to the aircraft construction and a crucially new for Uzbekistan motor-car industry as well as radio-electronics, electrotechnical, oil-chemical and other advanced industries which provide manufacturing equipment for light and food industries, small agricultural mechanization devices and the consumer goods. This is a clue to enter the world markets.

Development of these crucial avenues for the sectoral structural policies and finding the appropriate investments for their implementation is the important source for the further economic growth. It is a duty of the state to back up these priorities. Their reproduction in the country will ensure creation and development of the key infrastructure essential for the economic development.

At the second phase of the reformation process deep advanced developments in the agriculture and agro-industrial complex as a whole is of the most important priority. They should be aimed at the radical solution of food problem, at deeper procession of the agricultural raw materials and setting up small compact enterprises in the country-side, at development of the production and social infrastructure in the rural area to improve the living standards of the village population.

Structural policies in the agriculture are being implemented through the most efficient utilization of crop areas in accordance with the peculiarities of each particular zone. Along with cotton, seed farming and potato farming can be related to the key sectors. Implementation of measures on reorganization of the agricultural production structure will enable Uzbekistan to ensure not only the accelerated development of the most important agricultural crops and foodstuffs but to eliminate economic dependence of the country on the imported food and fodder grain, margarine products, food alcohol and other most important goods as well.

It is essential that the local fodder production should be significantly strengthened. It is necessary to reduce the import of fodder grain, soya-beans and others which would initially enable to stabilize and at a later stage to follow up with increasing output of meat and dairy products.

In-depth technical retooling of the processing sectors with the updated machinery and technologies, creation of the complete technological cycle for manufacturing quality competitive consumer goods, is the most important strategic objective. We place strong emphasis on deep procession of the most important agricultural resources such as cotton, silk, jute, fruit-and-vegetable products, viti-culture products, development of the light industry related sectors. We have made our aim to bring the share of the cotton-fibre being processed in the country up to the level of 28-30%. It is invisioned to have the output of dried fruit, raisins and dried vegetables being significantly increased. The baby food production requires special attention.

Setting up new processing capacities will enable extensively develop such labour intensive sectors of the production as spinning, weaving and decoration ones, to develop knitted-wear, textile and clothing industries, to widen the range of finished goods.

We must learn to trade not raw materials, not cheap half-finished goods but rather modern marketable finished products.

At the second phase of the reformation process improving land fertility becomes one of the most important, critical avenues for the development of the agricultural production. This is the reason why investments in agriculture must be made just in land reconstruction, in development of new irrigated lands, improvement of their agrochemical and amelioration state, in the development of irrigation and drainage networks. When we have fertile lands with high return then there will come foreign investments which would enable us to get involved in the intensification of the agricultural production and procession of the agricultural raw materials.

For the solution of the problems of stabilization and dynamic economic growth in the transition period special attention must be attached to the priority development of the production infrastructure sectors i.e. communications and transportation networks. Speaking of communication networks it is important to note that by virtue of Uzbekistan being a land-locked country, the issues relating to the development of the transportation and communication networks are gaining in priority, strategic and vital importance.

Infrastructure complex is a foundation, the whole structure of our economy is based upon. Good functioning of the whole national economy complex of the country, its efficacy, as well as possibility to attract and develop foreign investments, entirely depend on the status and level of development of the infrastructure's network.

It is the production transportation and communications infrastructure in first turn which give promotion to our goods and services in the world market, have impact on their competitiveness and at the same time serve the channel for obtaining essential information, raw materials, components, updated technologies and machinery.

This is the reason why we have to back up the production infrastructure sectors in every possible way, to allocate the necessary material and foreign exchange funds for their development, although they are scares, to promote attraction of foreign investments in above industries in the most efficient way. In the not too distant future already we are supposed to reach the international standards in term of the level of development of the telecommunication networks. Uzbekistan has no future without the well-developed communication system. And we must clearly realize this.

Enhancing social orientation of the economy with a view to saturate the Republican consumer market with the domestically produced food and consumer goods is the priority of structural transformations. Accelerated development of the labour intensive industries and services, allocation and overtaking development of small enterprises in the rural area, encouraging entrepreneurship, revival of handicraft will enable us not only to resolve the most important for the country problem of reconciliation of the manpower growth and jobs availability but to significantly expand scales and ranges of marketable consumer goods and services. Structural policies in the non-production sphere must be tied up to the solution of problems relating to strengthening material base of the health care, public education and culture, increasing of the level of social improvement of the cities, populated areas and villages, their gasification and water supply especially, in the country-side.

To fully supply population of the country with finished pharmaceuticals, it would be essential to set up a large-scale production of scarce medicines. Accelerated development of the pharmaceutical industry would be required for this purpose. Today Uzbekistan is the sole producer in the CIS of the rare pharmaceuticals, vaccines and serums which are widely known in the world market.

International travel becomes increasingly leading sector of the economy, important sources for replenishing foreign exchange revenues. Therefore consruction of the comfortable hotels, campings, developed tourism infrastructure, resort areas should be continued further on. Special attention should be attached to the restoration of the national-historical and cultural monuments serving the special significance for inviting foreign tourists, but first and foremost, for the revival of the values of the people, upbringing of the younger generation.

Territorial aspect is important for implementing the structural policies, because only through the development of production and social infrastructure in the economically undeveloped regions, optimal allocation of productive forces over there, it would become possible to eliminate territorial disproportions that have taken shape in the standards of living of people and to ensure the integrated and efficient utilization of resources and production capacities.

Implementation of structural reorganization of economy is inextricably entwined with maintaining active investment policies. Development and deepening of the investment base is the most important condition for the reform's strategy. Mapped out avenues of the structural reorganization of the economy, expansion of the export potential will be actually implemented providing strong investment policy be maintained. For this purpose all sources of investments, both domestic and external, including foreign loans and direct investments should be involved.

Today large-scale inviting foreign investments, including foreign capital are regarded as the necessary condition for achieving goals of structural reorganization of national economy. Attraction of foreign capital is planned in the form of direct investments, state loans, investment or credit resources to be advanced by the international finance and economic institutions and donor-countries. We concentrate mainly on attracting the foreign capital to back up implementation of the specific investment projects.

Today quite a few foreign firms and companies are willing to collaborate with us. It is important to learn to be wise in using these opportunities. It is expedient to import new technologies and to intensify construction of small quick return enterprises. For implementation of this priority objective it would be essential to conduct open doors policy for foreign investors, to further liberalize foreign trade activities, improve convertibility facility of incomes by foreign investors, to enhance guarantees to be offered to them.

Setting up an enterprise jointly with a foreign investor is one of the promising ways to achieve this goal. I want to reiterate again: an enterprise or an entrepreneur who has no relations with foreign partner, has no future.

But at the same time for achieving the major goal of the structural transformation we cannot rely upon foreign investments only, it is necessary to find out and to mobilize domestic reserves and investment sources.

In so doing serious attention should be attached to our untapped reserves. A considerable amount of the GOP goes for consumption, and just minor portion remains for accumulation. This can be given explanation under the present complicated conditions, but it cannot be regarded as a policy to be pursued in the nearest future. We must be clear in our mind that there will be no future without accumulation. We are doomed to mark time without accumulation and development of production.

And at this point changing psychology and attitude towards this issue would be required on the side of enterprises. To live for the day, not having essential reserves is unpromising.

Foreign investments will come when we ourselves and for ourselves make the appropriate accumulations to be served as the source of investments for the development of leading and, in the first turn, key sectors. Foreign investments are generally made in quick return ventures. Foreign investors to a lesser extent are worried about solution of our critical problems of structural transformations, priority development of the capital consuming, bringing no huge profit but essentially important sectors and productions of the country. That's why we have to find out sources of investments of our own for the development of the key sectors, for ensuring economic independence.

For these purposes one of the important objectives of the state at the second phase of the economic reform is becoming creation of the strong encouragement facility to intensify investment activities of enterprises and population at the expense of introduction of the soft taxation to be levied on means to be designed for investing into production and introduction of other measures as well.

Implementation of the integrated and goal-directed structural policies at the second phase of the reformation process, backing it up with necessary investments would enable us in the nearest future to achieve deep-rooted developments in the intergrated and wise utilization of agricultural and mineral resources, to set up new industries of specialization in the country along with the traditional ones i.e. oil mining and oil refining, moto-car building, electronics industry, instrument-making, foreign travel, seed-farming and fodder production as well as many others.

Mapped out avenues of the industrial development being coupled with the structural transformations in the agricultural production, with the dynamic development of the communication network and services, social sphere as a whole will create necessary conditions for the well-balanced functioning of the economy, achieving rational employment of the population and improvement of its well-being.

Thefore, the major objective during the whole transition period is to implement the in-depth structural reorganization of the whole national economy. To create such a structure that would enable us to ensure economic and political independence of Uzbekistan with consideration for all our resources.

2.5. OUR GOAL IS THE FORMATION OF THE DEMOCRATIC STATE WITH STRONG SOCIAL GUARANTEES

Economic policy underway in Uzbekistan that is embodied in the deep-rooted economic reform, in the long run is aimed at the formation of the sound material basis for democratic transformations, creation of mighty law governed sovereign state. Our objective is to construct the democratic, fair and civic society. This is our cherished dream, our strategy. This is the point of the general ideology and universal programme for national renaissance and development.

Building democratic society completely meets the interests of the multinational people of Uzbekistan who associate their dreams of freedom, happiness and well-being with the reforms that are taking place in all areas of social life. And our duty is to make their expectations come true. Our intention is to build a society of the truly free people.

What is the purpose of all reforms in the long run? For whom in first turn shall we erect the building of the renewed democratic society? For our people, of course, for our children.

We have been repeatedly emphasizing that implementation of the reform and deep-rooted systemic transformation is not an end in itself. The impact of these reforms on the people is the most important to us. What changes for the better will take place in the life of the people? To what extent their life becomes richer and more beautiful? To what extent a person feels free to pursue his own labour, his own destiny, his own nation?

Therefore an individual, a citizen of the sovereign Uzbekistan is in the focus of our versatile activities relating to the reformating and renewal of the society. Reforms are meant to provide the chance for an individual to show his or her abilities, talent and personal qualities. All transformations in the economic and political life are just subordinated to achieving the supreme goal i.e. to make life of every individual better more worthwhile and spiritually richer.

On the other hand, targets, dynamics and efficiency of the reforming processes entirely depend upon concrete persons. The success of our reforms, the future of our country will depend on what kind of person he or she will be in the nearest future, what spiritual,— cultural and moral values he or she will be devoted to.

This is the reason why we are striving to build such a state that would meet both the generally recognized democratic principles and standards and the traditional moral values of our people. The democratic state we are building now should proceed from the mentality of our people who are unique in terms of their spiritual values and lofty feeling of social justice, striving for enlightenment and education. These traits have been taken shape mainly under the effect of the Oriental philosophy, Islamic philosophy, to the development of which the Uzbek people have made their invaluable, generally recognized contribution.

The independence has been provided the historic opportunity, while shaping up the statehood, to apply to the roots of our culture, to the enourmous spiritual heritage to be cognized, in order to perceive and develop the best what we have in our past. Profound and comprehensive scrutiny of the achievements of the oriental civilization, culture and spiritual wealth of our forerunners opens up a possibility for us to know better culture, mode of living, traditions and customs of our ancient people. Our duty is to replenish national spiritual treasury with new names and works by our great predecessors-philosophers, scholars, creators of beauty.

Having liberated spiritual values from the ideological dogmas, we could open up a wide road for the renaissance of national self-awareness, shaping up and development of free philosophy and national ideology. Next comes the objective for our people to be self-confident, to be able to change their lives for the better after they have got enriched with knowledge.

Henceforth, we will display the maximum care of the renaissance, preservation, enhancing and development of the moral, spiritual and cultural achievements of the nation to be able to serve the guarantor for the diversity and distinct culture of Uzbekistan, guarantor for the democratic transformation.

Social construction processes and economic development should be meshed with spiritual improvement and morals. Our policy relies upon this and we would be consistent in conducting such type of policies, where there is no confidence, no enthusiasm, there is no creative activities.

The democratic transformation can be achieved through the intricate everyday work in the material and spiritual spheres. It is important to achieve that the necessity for democratic transformation be not only realized by the population but be taken by them as the only way to true freedom, independence and well-being.

True democracy is measured by the level of the superiority of law, range of rights and freedoms granted, by the strength of the social guarantees. Any state, especially the one striving for true democracy is supposed to be able to safely protect the interests of its people, honour and dignity of its citizens, their lives and freedoms.

Successful solution of the social problems, provision of reliable social guarantees, enhancing labour incentives would create solid social support for the implementation of the reforms, would serve to guarantee their irreversible character.

Our goal is to construct not just a democratic society as it is but rather a fair democratic society. Striving for justice is the most important characteristic feature of the mentality of our people. The whole system of economic and social relations should be permeated with the idea of justice to be reflected in the mechanism of social support. We will not be able to build a democratic, mighty state without considering this.

We have no right to allow an abrupt stratification of the society into the very rich and the very poor. It would be important to intensify the shift to the targeted social safety net and support to be provided to the most needy population — children, single, elderly and disabled. Therefore, at the second stage of the reform there will be pursued the policy aimed at the improvement of the social support system, finalizing shaping up the efficient facility for social protection of the population. Actual material support should be provided to the concrete families, but it should be a targeted support being offerred to those who actually need it and cannot survive in complicated transition times.

For the time being there were devised major principles and distribution channels for the material support to be provided by the state to the socially vulnerable strata of population.

Our society is special in terms of being relied upon the idea of collectivism, unity of common interests, public understanding of priority. Therefore, in the democratic system of the society, implementation of its key principles, and the social principle of justice in the first turn, the makhallya has the special role to play. For the time being the makhallya is being the best advised in terms of financial health of a family, range of its cultural and spiritual interests. The makhallya is the most just and trustworthy channel and social support facility for the population. It is designed to become the reliable support and efficient instrument to implement the reform in our society.

Therefore, it would be essential, henceforth, to enhance the role of the local administration in the solution of the urgent social problems, to back them up with the appropriate funds. It is a duty of a state to provide assistance in every possible way to the local administration to solve this most important social problem.

Along with this there should be enhanced the socially targeted character of the local administration and local governments' activities, of such recognized government institutions as khokimiyats. Today it is the khokimiyat that is responsible for ensuring uninterrupted functioning of structures with regards the population supply with consumer goods, municipal services and solution of the rational employment problems.

Therefore, khokimiyats are supposed to encourage and support, in every possible way, the establishment of small, compact enterprises to manufacture consumer goods and offer services, to maintain decentralized procurement of the most needed products. It is essential to arrange the reliable, uninterrupted sales of consumer goods, to enlarge their range, to ensure access of the wide strata of the population to them. Much attention should be given to the most convenient location of retail shops and service centres. The population should feel comfortable for the response to its vital needs.

The efforts by khokimiyats should be concentrated on adhering and strengthening the material basis for the social infrastructure. It is necessary to extensively provide various types of social services at the expense of privatization of certain social sphere premises and facilities, encouraging non-government, private property forms of social services and at the expense of improving activities by social institutions owned by the municipal bodies. The actual competitive environment should be shaped up not only in the production but in the social sphere as well. Organizations offerring services to the population, regardless of the forms of ownership, must struggle for their customers and improve service standards and quality. It is essential everywhere, in all areas of activities, in the social sphere in the first turn, to secure a consumer dictate, a dictate of a human being with his or her needs, over the producer of the material wealth and services.

The most important priority in the khokimiyats' activities still remains the supply of the populated areas, villages and settlements with natural gas and drinking water. A considerable progress has been achieved, but there still remain quite a few villages where basic public utilities are yet not available. This disadvantage needs to be immediately eliminated. The urban population and the population of the remote villages should enjoy equal rights in terms of using electricity, drinking water, natural gas and other public utilities. For these purposes local khokimiyats are supposed to find the appropriate funds, to invite all concerned enterprises and agencies for the solution of this problem. Establishing broad social and production infrastructure in the country-side will enable us to invite necessary funds to create new job places, setting up new production capacities and, eventually, to solve the wide range of social problems, to improve living conditions of the rural population.

Our objective is to set up such an institutional mechanism that would secure equal starting possibilities for everybody so that they could display and implement their abilities and satisfy their needs.

Every honestly working person must have enough means to support his family, to have equal rights in terms of education, medical services, social security. But at the same time everyone's position in the society must be determined by his or her willingness and ability to work.

The strong social policy is meant not only for protecting people's interests during the complicated transition period but rather for creating strong incentives for efficient labour, in establishing guaranteed right of free economic choice and free enterprise, for improving work and social activities of the population. Implementation of the transition-to-market programme in social terms would rely upon, first and foremost, on the economically active strata of population whose energy, enthusiasm, orientation to changes would facilitate establishing new economic relations, the soonest recovery of the drop in the production rise in the economy.

Provision of more work incentives, establishing conditions for creative and work potential of everybody to be displayed is the most critical task of the second phase of the reformation process. Economic relations with a reliance on the combination of the anyone's economic freedom with his or her economic responsibility for own well-being and well-being of the whole family would be needed. The relations would be required to rely on the own creative abilities and possibilities is the sole and stable source of his or her well-being.

As this takes place every citizen of Uzbekistan should be ensured the property right, right of full freedom to carry out the economic activities, right of freedom to choose in respect of the area and forms of application for his labour in terms of his everyday life and from the legislative point of view.

Solution of the problems relating to the employment of the able-bodied population is closely connected with the realization of the right to work, possibility to be involved in the entrepreneurship activities and to earn incomes. In Uzbekistan that is different in terms of its population structure and high birth rates, the employment issues have always been and still remain among the priorities.

Solution of this problem can be achieved at the expense of:

— **first**, encouraging development of private small enterprises involved in versatile activities, related mainly to processing agricultural raw materials, manufacturing consumer goods, building materials from local raw materials as well as at the expense of creating conditions for extensive private enterprise;

— **second**, accelerated development of services, in the country-side particularly by offerring wider choices of municipal and construction services to the population. Services are untapped reserves able to absorb and to provide jobs not only to those released, but basically to all;

— **third**, significant improvement of refreshing and retraining system for those released. There should be set up the developed network of the special consultancy and training centres, business-schools which would provide released persons and those unqualified with new profession to meet the market conditions and changing economic structure as well as to assist them in terms of the economic and psychological adaptation to the changes in their lives;

— **and finally**, those who cannot be temporarily employed, must be provided the appropriate social protection on behalf of the state, and have guaranteed sources to ensure their vital needs.

Solution of unemployment problems affects women's interests, first of all. They are more sensitive and socially vulnerable in terms of employment. We are supposed to change position of women in the society and family. **Attitude towards women should be the measure of spiritual and moral maturity of our society.**

We are supposed to pay more attention to organization of the labour and every-day life of our women, to create appropriate conditions for them to be able to combine house-keeping with an active involvement into the social production. It would be essential to promote women to higher positions, to assign them with independent and responsible missions, to give them an opportunity to fully display their professional and spiritual potential.

It would be important to improve the prestige of a woman-mother, to give them their due for their work, for upbringing physically fit, spiritually rich and integrated generation. Taking care of mother and her child is the holy duty of a state. And we must do our utmost to ensure mothers and children of Uzbekistan to become comfortably off, healthy, happy, so that they could feel optimistic about their future.

And for this purpose, the improvement of the public health care has the special role to play. It requires to be not only radically reformed, but technically updated, strengthened and equipped with advanced diagnostic devices and qualified medical staff. In this respect priority must be given to the regional multi-profiled hospitals and country-sided medical institutions designed to bring the preventive treatment up to the higher level.

The whole preventive treatment and diagnostic work, children vaccination system, medical and epidemiological services need to be brought up to the qualitatively new level. Once and for all we must put barriers for epidemics not to be proliferated in the territory of Uzbekistan, to learn to diagnose a disease in its early stage, to combat it in a most efficient way by applying the updated methods, to improve efficiency of the hospitals' network.

When assessing health care status we had better refuse quantitative indicators such as a number of beds and medical institutions, number of doctors in favour of reliance upon qualitative indicators trying to achieve increasing the length of the population's life, reducing infants' and mothers' mortality rates, reducing infectious, heart- and -vuscular and other widespread deseases as well. Only physically fit and healthy population would be able to perform those profound changes which are in the core of our large-scale programme of the renewal and progress. We are supposed to promote comprehensive improvement of our people's health through developing all sorts of medical services to be based on both state and private ownership, at the expense of the medical insurance networks.

Achieving our goals, building new democratic society, the future of the reform will depend on the available intellectual capability, cultural and professional level of our youth, its ideals and spiritual values. Therefore, one of our priorities is to improve the educational level of the population, up-bringing of the younger generation to be able to implement the concept of the national reneissance.

Only well-educated, educated and professional persons can be economically free and reliable proponents of the crucial economic transformation. Awaring this truth should lie in the basis of the whole development process of the spiritual and cultural life of the people, in the renewal of the whole system of education.

We should remember that only that country, that nation can achieve great future, prosperity and well-being which would be able to train knowledgeable, professional and energetic persons, true patriots of their country, the country which would provide them with huge spiritual legacy of the great national culture and give them access to the world treasury of science and culture.

Path to the national reneissance lies through the high level education and culture. This is the reason why the level of education and professional training should become the measure of progress of our social development on the threshold of the 21st century. This is the best guarantee that the implementation of the mapped out reforms' deal will be successful, this is exactly the avenue which would bring high returns on the funds invested.

This is our responsibility to assist in creating conditions for our young boys and girls to acquire the amount of knowledge necessary for an educated person, to absorb cultural, moral, ethic and spiritual values that would enable them to easily assimilate with new conditions, to become active participants in the building of their removed country and reformation process.

It would be essential to reorganize the whole system of national education more resolutely and keep higher pace with it. Contemporary conditions require to treat the system of public education as one chain of all its links, each of them is responsible either for pre-school training of children, high school, special or professional training, spiritual and moral shaping up young people as personalities, their physical improvement as well. Only such a system can serve the basis for upbringing physically and spiritually healthy generation that would be able to complete the noble construction of a new prosperous society commenced today by their parents.

For this purpose it would be required to significantly strengthen the secondary schooling, the system of higher and specialized education, to up-date curricula, to enrich them with, the world treasury of knowledge, to arrange publications of the up-dated text-books and reference books, to revive the authority of the teachers, to make their work prestigious and highly paid.

Special attention should be paid to the organization of the out-of-school work amongst children, strengthening material base and development of social and cultural institutions such as libraries, theatres, museums, exhibition halls and others called upon to shape up high culture and education, kindness and honesty, integrity with young generation. **Full commercialization of culture, the whole show — bussiness cannot be tolerated to prevent cultivating primitive, vulgar concept of the market relations, values of life, prosperity and ways of achieving this prosperity among the youth.**

Democratic society is, first of all, a civic society. The highest purport of the true democracy is the reconciliation of interperson, ethnic, state and political relations pursuing peace and concord between an individual and society, society and state power.

Over its many-century history Uzbekistan has always been and still remains one of the unique states where multinational composition of population has taken shape and has been developing dynamically since the olden days. All citizens of the country irrespective of their nationality, constitute the integrated and single sovereign people of Uzbekistan.

We oppose making any distinctions on the basis of nationality. There are no big or small nations in the world. Every nation is special in terms of the settled ancient traditions, rich historic legacy, unity of the national spirit, original culture. **The holy duty of the Uzbeks as the national majority of the country is not only to revive their mother tongue, their national culture and history but be responsible for the future of the national minorities in the country, for preserving their original culture and spiritual values, granting equal conditions and possibilities for self-development and displaying their abilities.**

Civil peace, ethnic concord and friendship, striving for maintaining and cementing them have always been and will be distinguishing features of our people who hand down these qualities from generation to generation. Uzbekistan will remain a true democratic, international state with strong social guarantees henceforth.

In accordance with the developed principles and priorities, Uzbekistan consistently and steadily is moving on the own path of renewal and progress. One can actually feel the first outcomes of the reformation processes in all spheres of social life. State and political system of our young sovereign Uzbekistan has acquired new modern democratic features. For the first time in the history of the country Oliy Majlis — the Parliament of the country — has been elected on a multi-party basis. Such generally recognized democratic standards as freedom of will, freedom of speech, conscience and religion are becoming firmly established in our life.

Civil peace, ethnic concord, social stability make our country special compared to the many post-socialist countries, this makes us alike with the highly developed, civilized democratic states and opens up the way for the wide-scale integration into the world community.

Democratization of social life is directly expressed in strengthening and increasing role of the local governments and administrations, i.e. regional, city and district khokimiyats for the solution of the most critical problems of national economy. The influence of the self-governing organs such as makhallyas has considerably increased in the course of implementing the principles of social justice. In the administration system more freedom was given to the lower economic agents, enterprises themselves, their voluntary associations. The role of the state and state administrative organs is undergoing the crucial changes. They are more focussed on their main functions and objectives: determining strategy and monitoring over its implementation, ensuring defence capacity and security of the country, maintaining active foreign policies, shaping up framework conditions for social and economic-production activities.

In the economic sphere reformation process has laid a foundation for the new market relations, revealed space for free economic activities, initiative and enterprise. There have been made actual steps for overcoming the drop of production, stabilization of the economic and financial position of the country, improving distortions in the economy which have been allowed in the previous decades.

With regards to social and spiritual sphere concerned, in the course of reformation process there have been strengthened the social guarantees, the facilities for social protection of population which have been developed by us, have worked well, and did not allow the abrupt deterioration of living standards of the population within the complicated period of transition. Liberation from ideological dogmas has enabled us to know the history of our country and people better, to get the access to the spiritual values which have been created over many centuries, to realize the beauty and greatness of the mother tongue, all this served the basis for the national renaissance. Increasing spiritual values have enabled us to take a new approach towards values of life, evaluation of concept and objectives of social development and whole process of reformation and renewal.

In the history of our people there was started a new period. We have embarked upon the new phase of our development. The objectives of the second stage are made clear, they arise from what has been achieved and are aimed at deepening the reformation processes. We should be more advanced on the path of democratization of our society, building democratic, fair civil society with socially oriented and developed market economy.

The objective of the second stage of the reformation process is in strengthening democratic system of the country, in reinforcing the role of law and legal standards in the system of public life and economic activities, in the split of power functions amongst various links of the integral state administration system, in granting more rights and authorities to the local governments and local administrations, self-governing bodies. In the political life the pluralism, political tolerance and responsibility for the future of our people should be firmly established. In the course of realization of the economic reform, at its second stage it would be necessary to ensure the economic stability, to strenghthen the national currency, to intensify the processes of denationalization and privatization, to extensively commence creation of small private enterprises and to shape up real competitive environment. All this should serve a reliable basis for deep structural transformations, bringing economy up to the qualitatively new level which would ensure its entering in the world markets and integration into the world economic system.

The deal of reform which we have devised and are implementing, is widely welcomed by the largest international economic and finance institutions, by the world community, by the largest economically developed countries of the world; this makes us confident in the correctness of the path chosen, in the success of the implementation of the own model of transition to the market relations.

Implementation of the mapped out objectives and priorities of the second stage of the democratic and economic reform is closely connected with strengthening social guarantees and development of spiritual values and culture of our people. High spiritual values are the foundation for irreversible crucial changes, assertion of true democratic and civilized way of entering into the world economy.

For successful implementation of deepening reform process, it would be essential to consolidate the legal basis, to pass new laws which would encourage and provide guarantees for radical changes, it would be necessary to provide the national economy with the competent professionals who are devoted and true patriots of their motherland.

The success of the reform is in the hands of each of us, of all people of Uzbekistan. If we want our country be free, rich and prosperous, if we want our children be happy and well-to-do, we must do our utmost to accomplish the aims and tasks of the second stage of the reform process. It is called upon laying reliable foundation for the dynamic development of our country, strengthening of its might and authority in the world community. And our holy duty, holy responsibility before future generations is to achieve those goals.

CONTENTS

Foreword ... 3

Introduction ... 7

Part 1

RESULTS AND LESSONS OF THE FIRST STAGE OF ECONOMIC REFORM ... 15

1.1. Mechanism of Formation of Economic Reform's Strategy and Course ... 16

1.2. Establishment of a Legal Basis is an Important Result of the First Stage of Economic Reform ... 26

1.3. Privatization of State Property and Shaping of Multi-Structural Economy ... 38

1.4. Reformation of Agriculture and Formation of Agrarian Relations of a New Type ... 52

1.5. Institutional Transformations and Elimination of Administrative-Command System of Management ... 67

1.6. Liberalization of Prices and Shaping of Market Infrastructure ... 78

1.7. Liberalization of External Economic Activity and Integration With the World Economic Community ... 90

1.8. Ensurance of Reliable Social Guarantees is an Important Result of the First Stage of Reform ... 106

1.9. Spiritual and Moral Rejuvenation of Nation is a Social Foundation of Economic Reform ... 122

1.10. Securing Economic and Socio-Political Independence is the Main Result of the First Stage of Reform ... 134

Part 2

TASKS AND PRIORITIES OF THE SECOND STAGE OF ECONOMIC REFORM   149

2.1. Extension of the Privatization Process and Formation of the Competitive Environment is the Key Task of the New Stage of Economic Reform   155

2.2. Achieving Macro-Economic Stabilization is the Priority of the Economic Reform's Strategy   168

2.3. Strengthening National Currency is the Key Objective of the New Phase of the Economic Reform   186

2.4. Achieving Deep-Rooted Structural Transformations is the Major Condition for the Sustainable Economic Growth   195

2.5. Our Goal is the Formation of the Democratic State With Strong Social Guarantees   210

Ислам Абдуганиевич Каримов

**УЗБЕКИСТАН
ПО ПУТИ УГЛУБЛЕНИЯ
ЭКОНОМИЧЕСКИХ РЕФОРМ**

Переводчики: *Рахманов К. Р., Ставицкая Е. Б.*
Ответственная за выпуск С. *Катышева-Гришина*
Художник А. *Саибназаров*
Техн. редактор С. *Сабирова*

Сдано в набор 23.05.95. Подписано в печать 08.06.95.
Формат 84х108¹/32. Гарнитура "Таймс". Печать офсетная.
Усл. печ. л. 12,18. Уч. изд. л.10,15. Тираж 20000. Заказ 649.
Цена договорная.

Издательство "Ўзбекистон", 700129, Ташкент, ул. Навои, 30.
Изд. № 118—95.

Оригинал-макет изготовлен на базе технических и программных средств ОсОО "Ношир".

Отпечатано на арендном предприятии Ташполиграфкомбината Государственного комитета по печати Республики Узбекистан. 700129, Ташкент, ул. Навои, 30.